TOM MATO'S COLORING BOOK

JOE TROIA

MY NEPHEW WOULD NOT LET ME USE HIS COLORING BOOK, SO I MADE MY OWN!

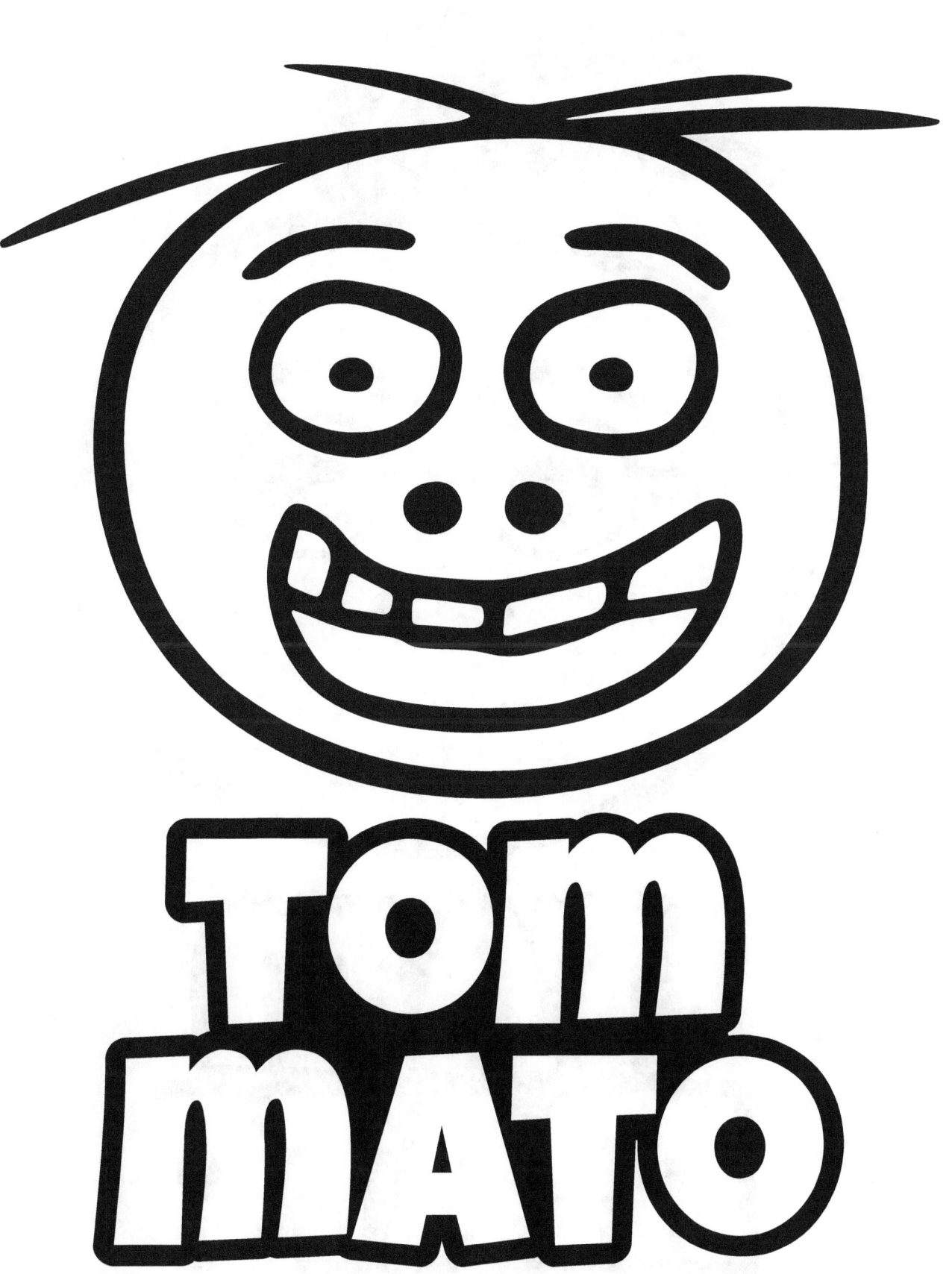

TOM
MATO

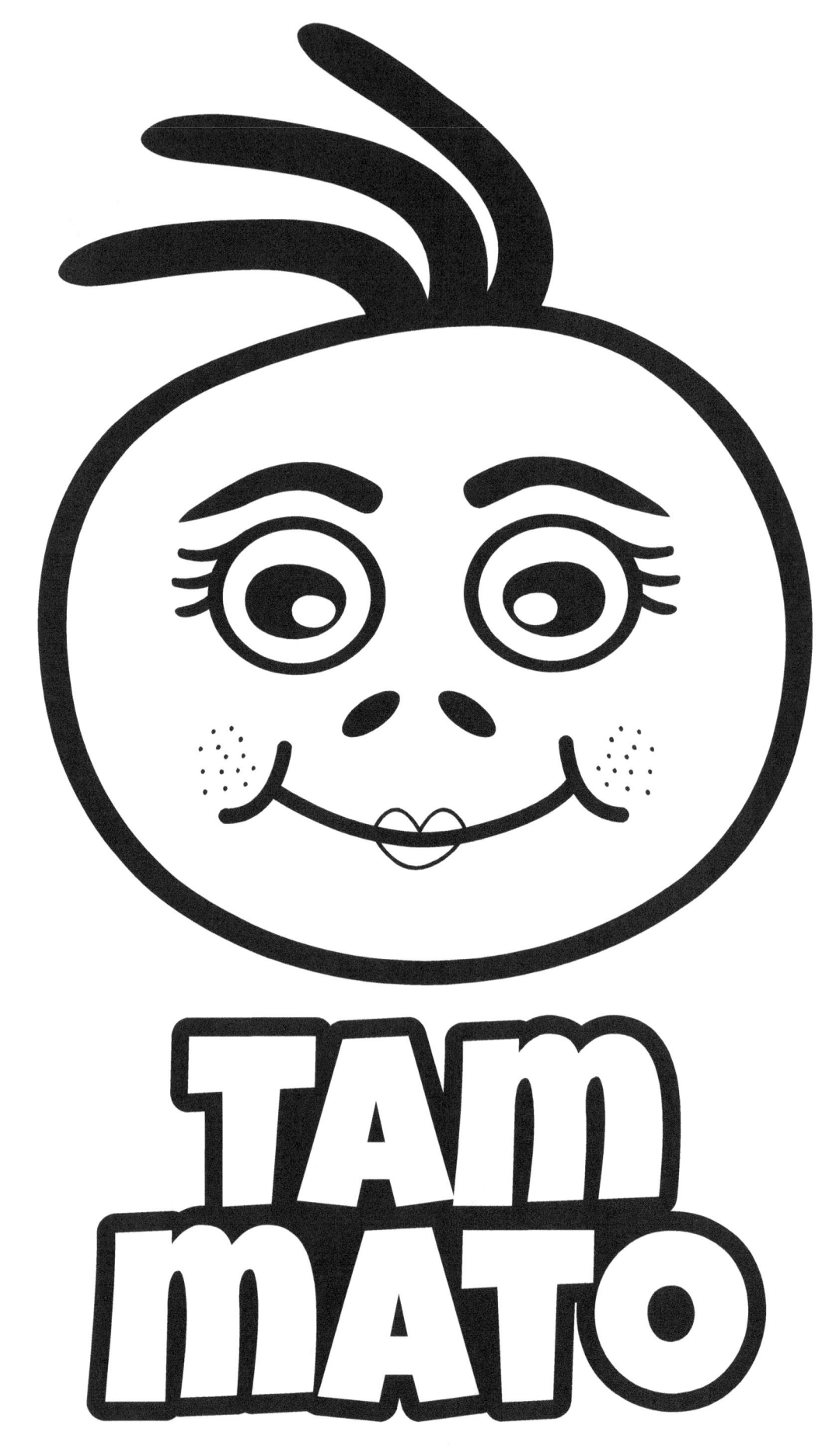

TAM
MATO

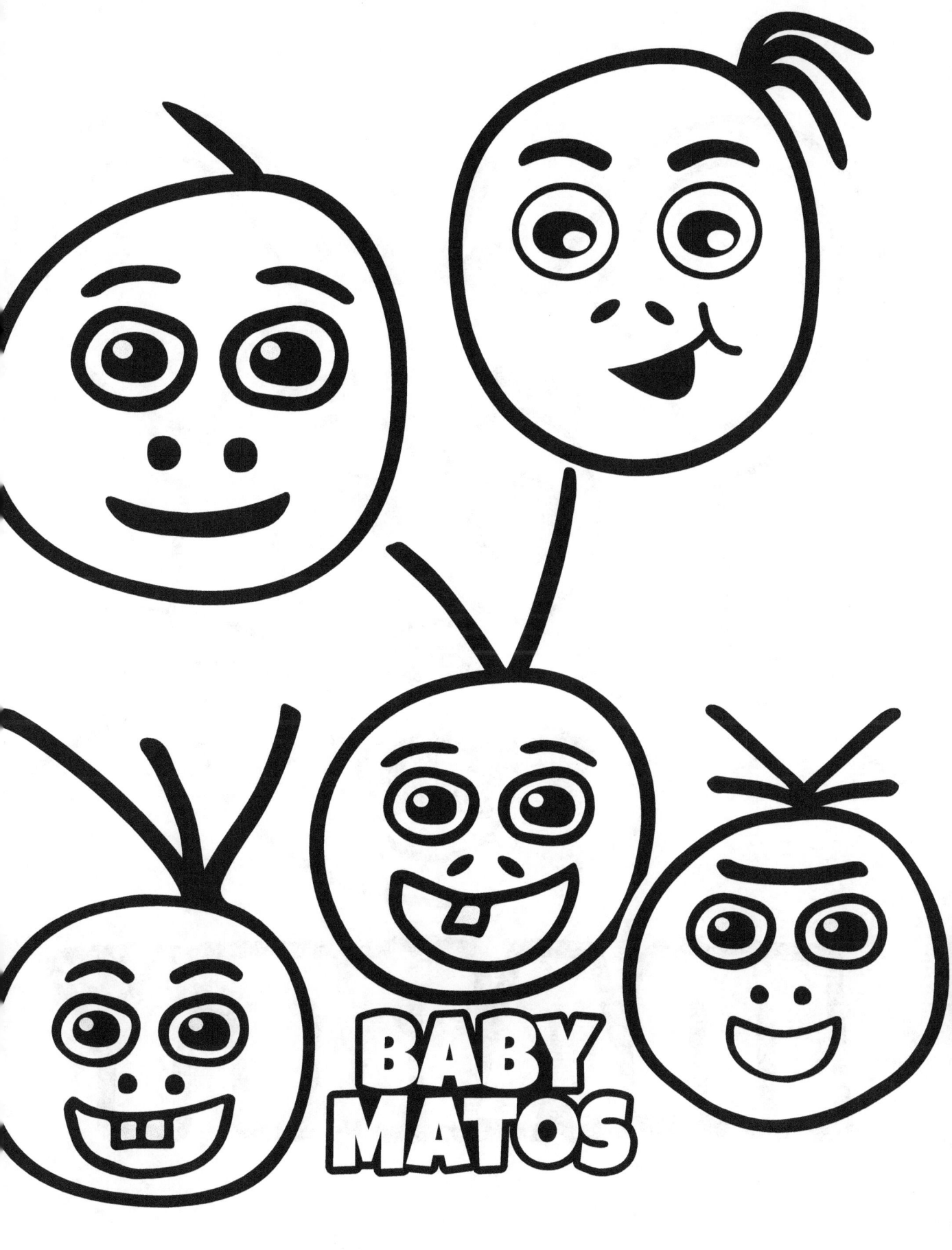

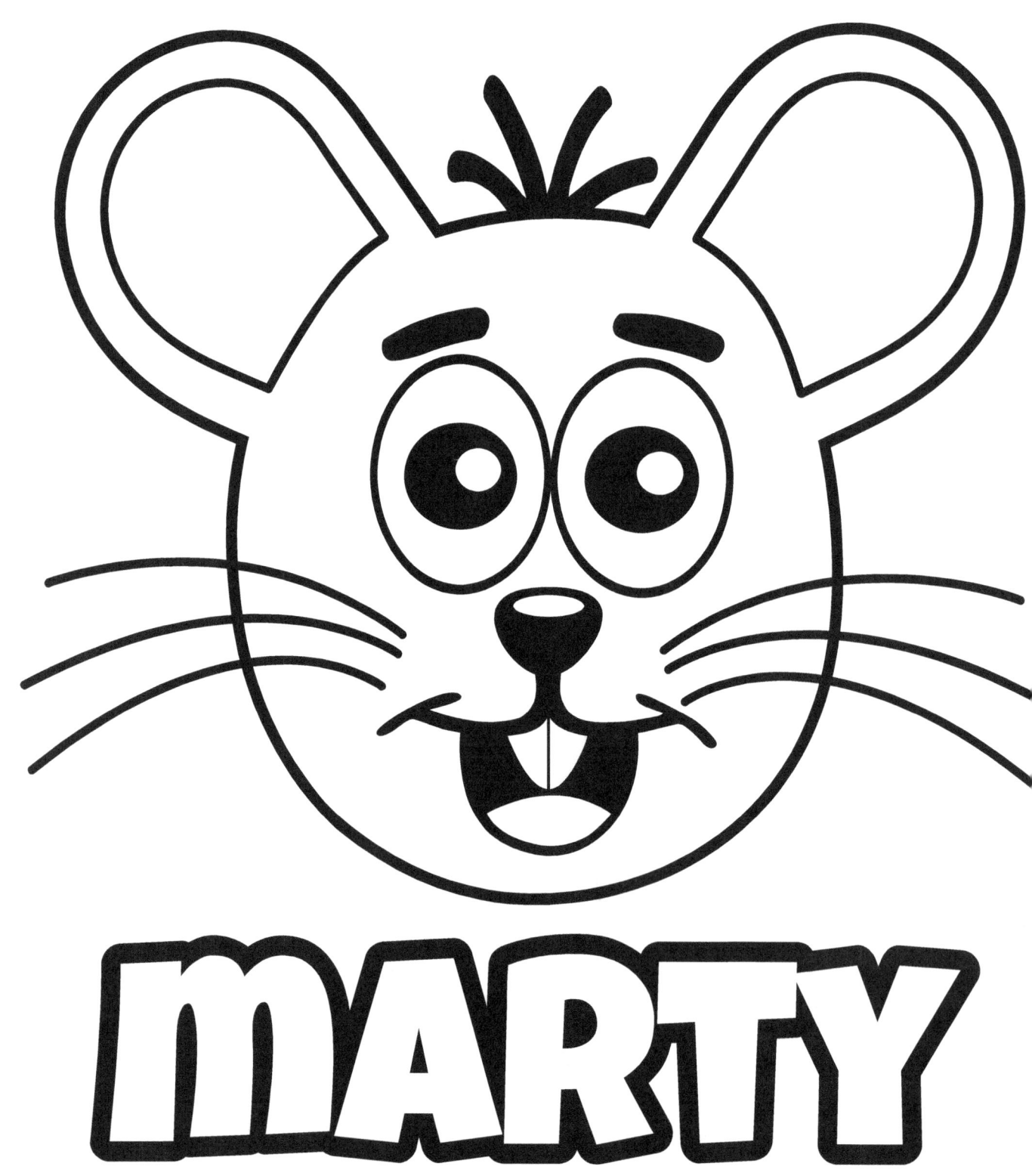

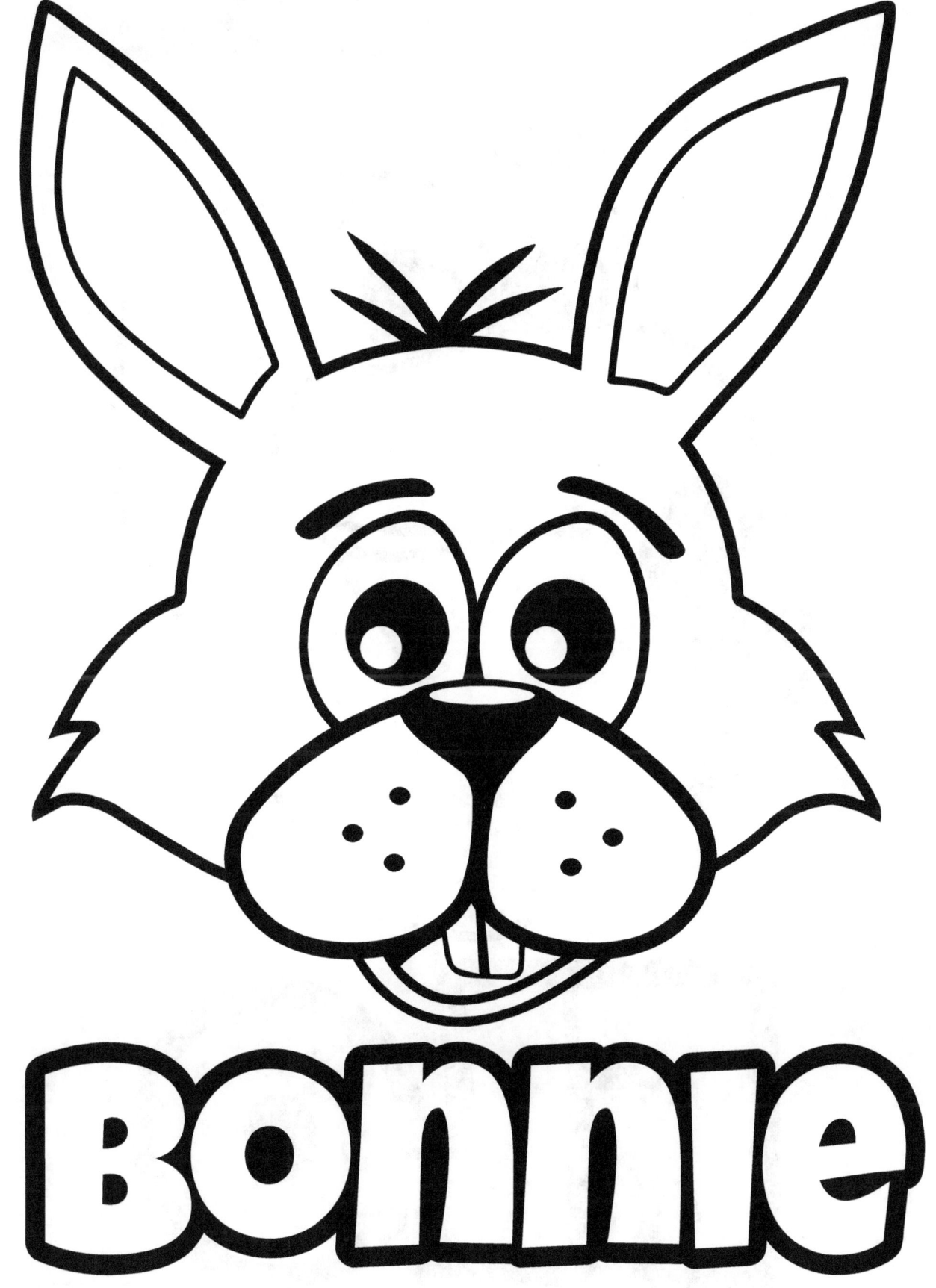

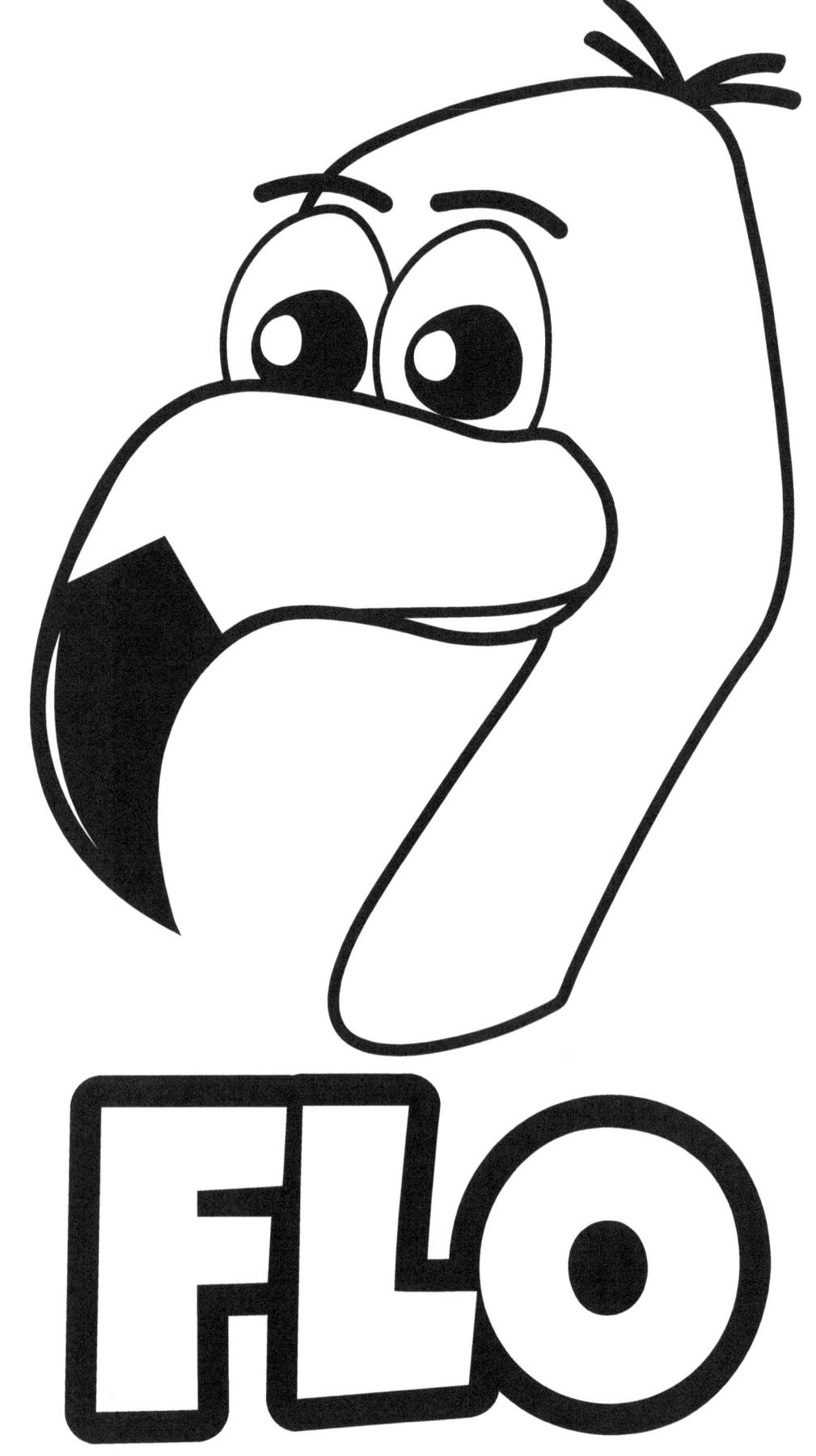

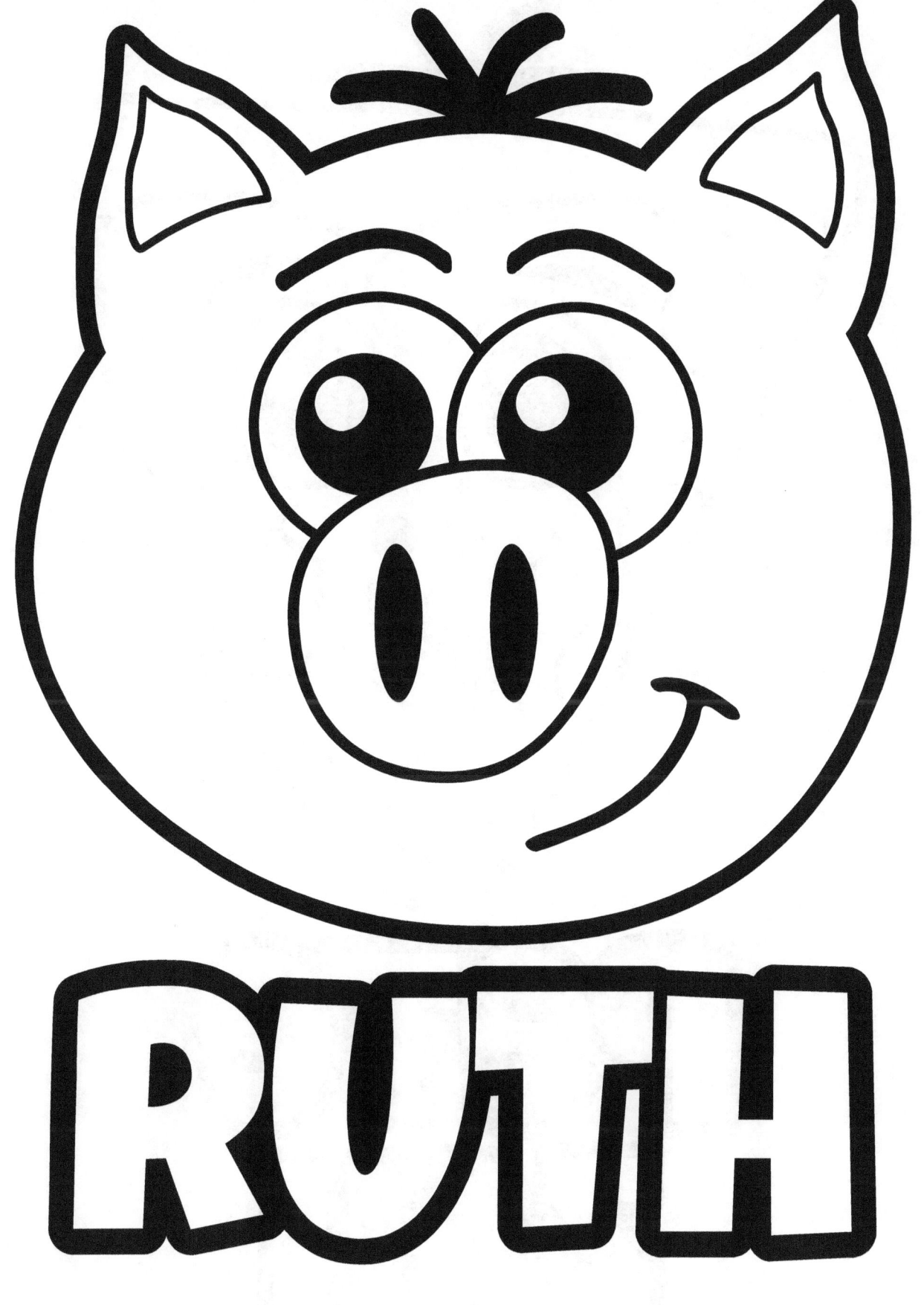

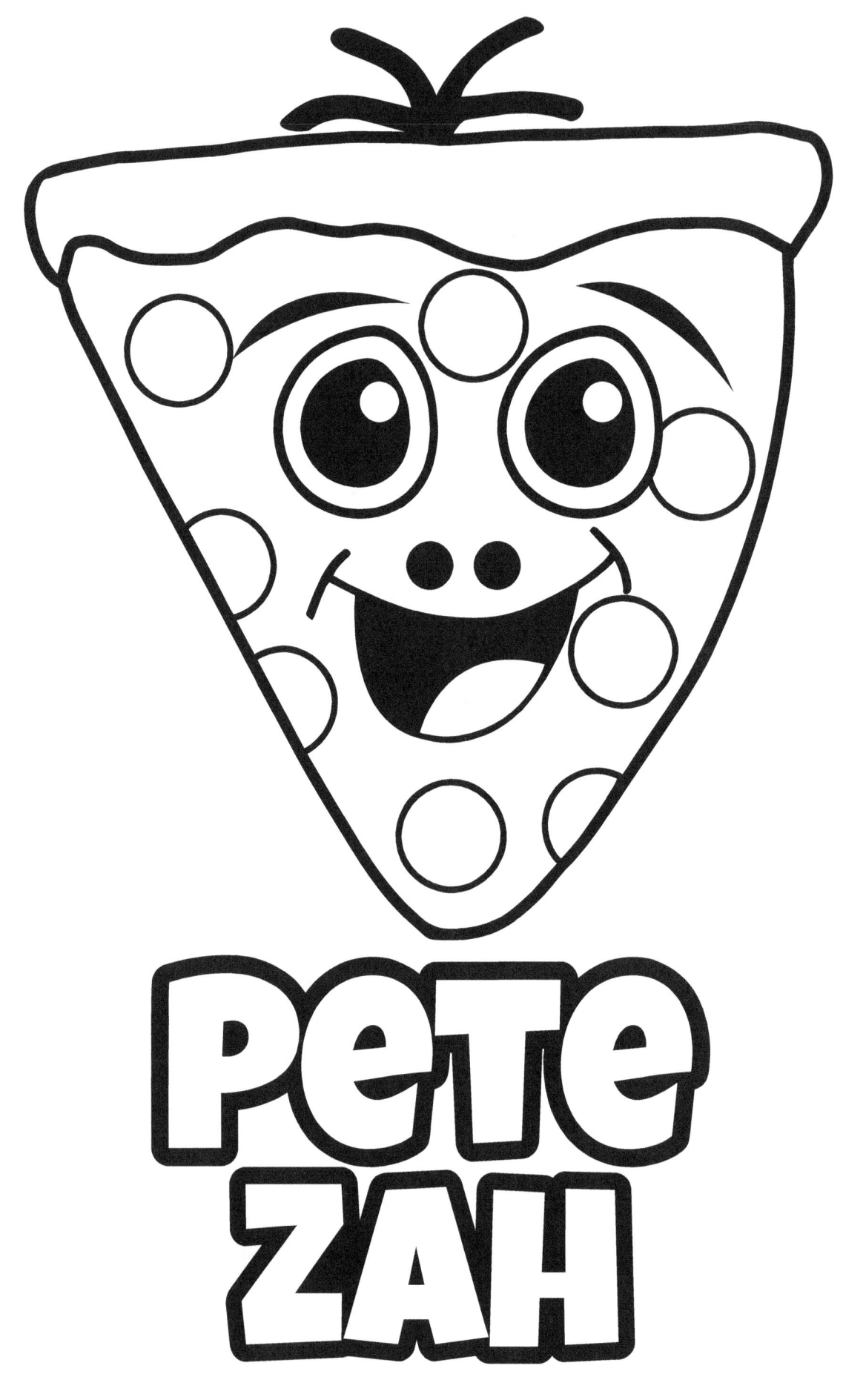

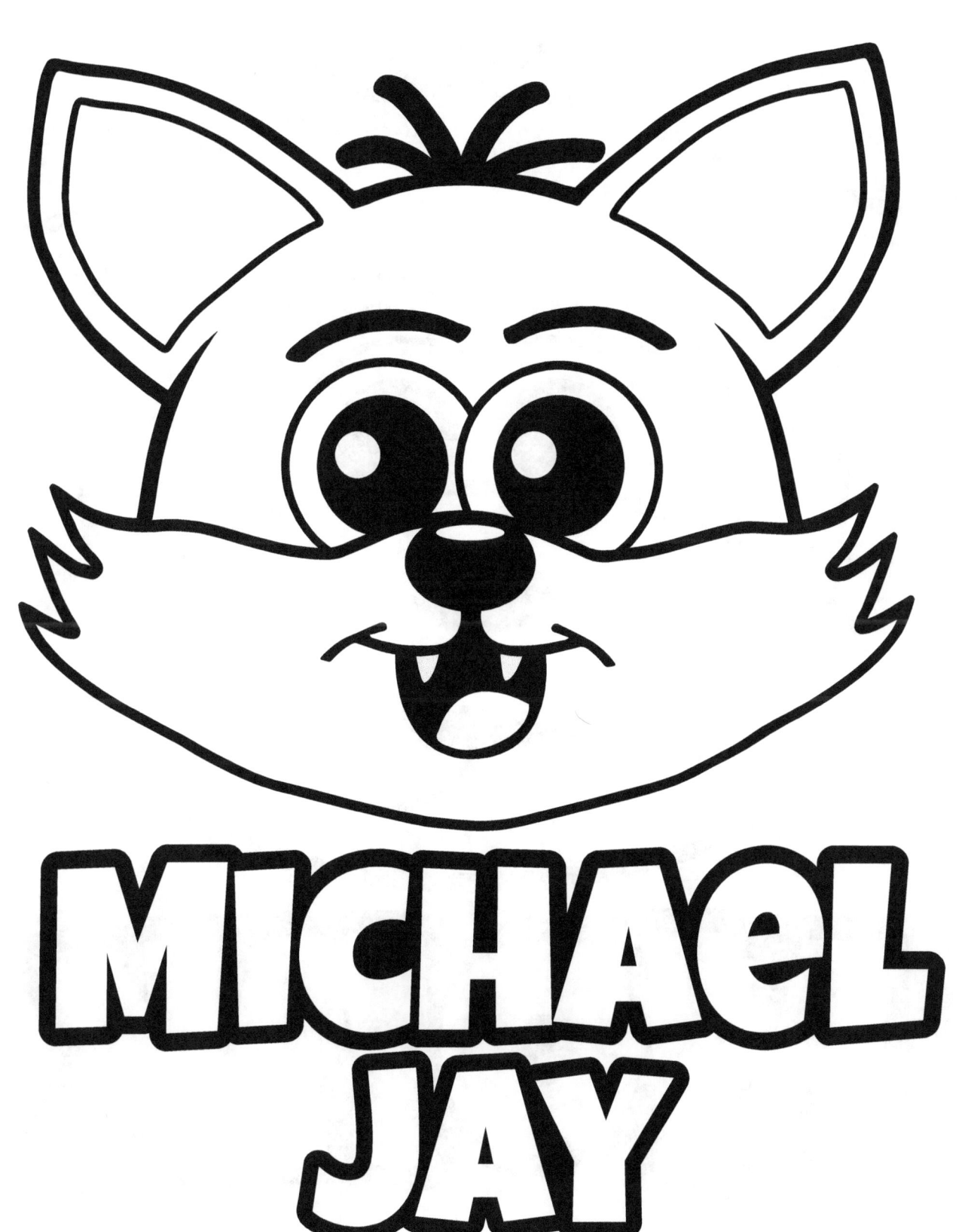

MICHAEL JAY

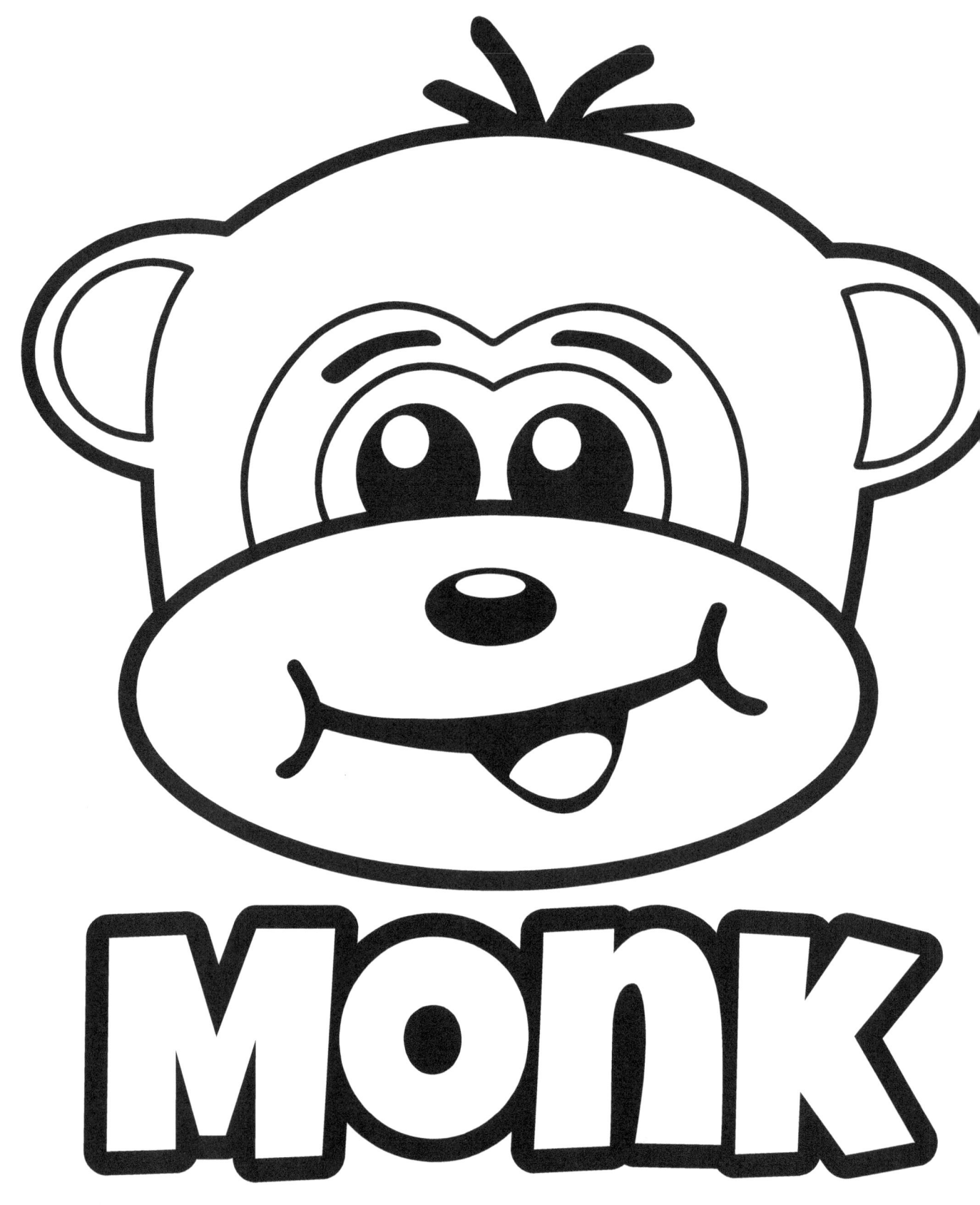

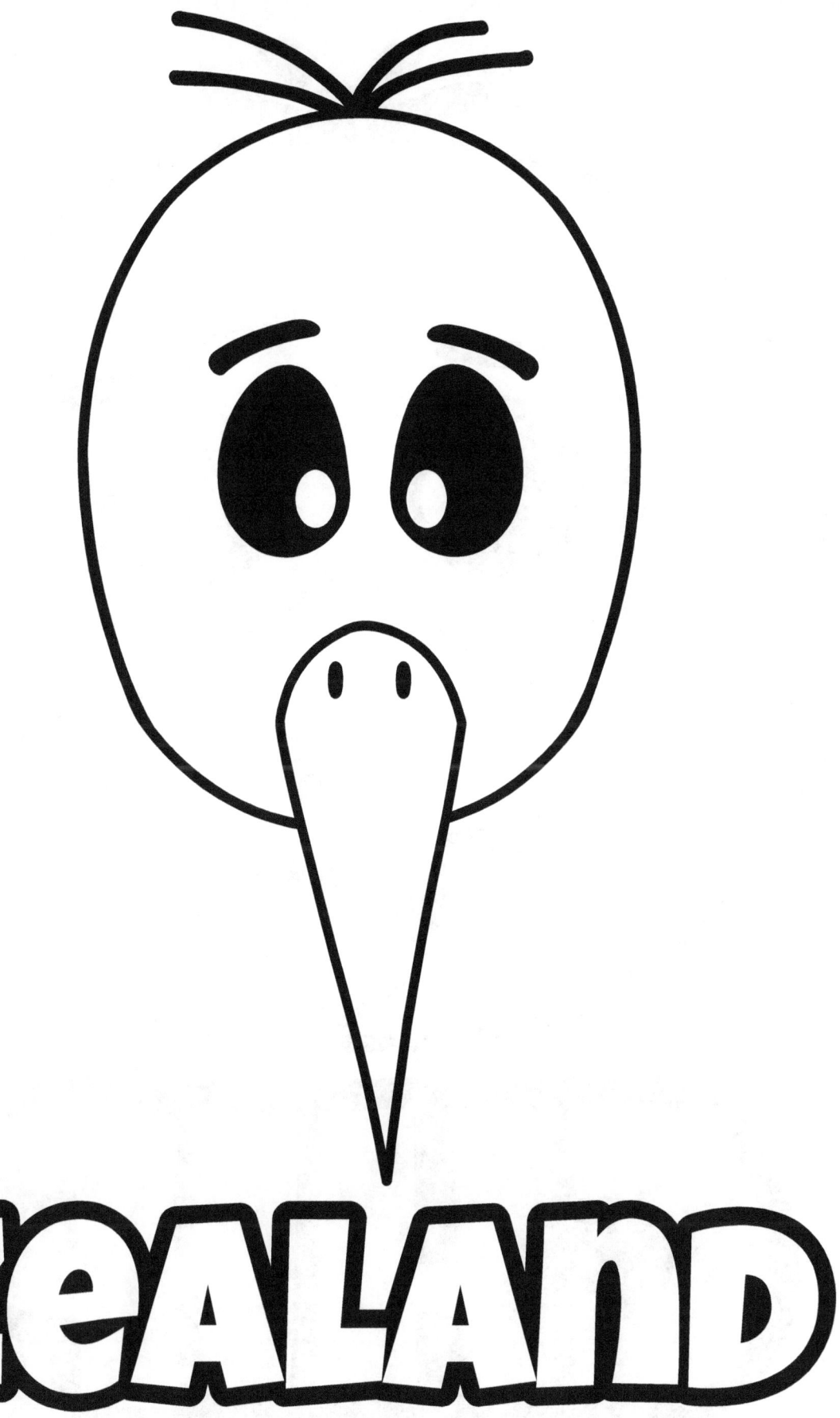

ZEALAND

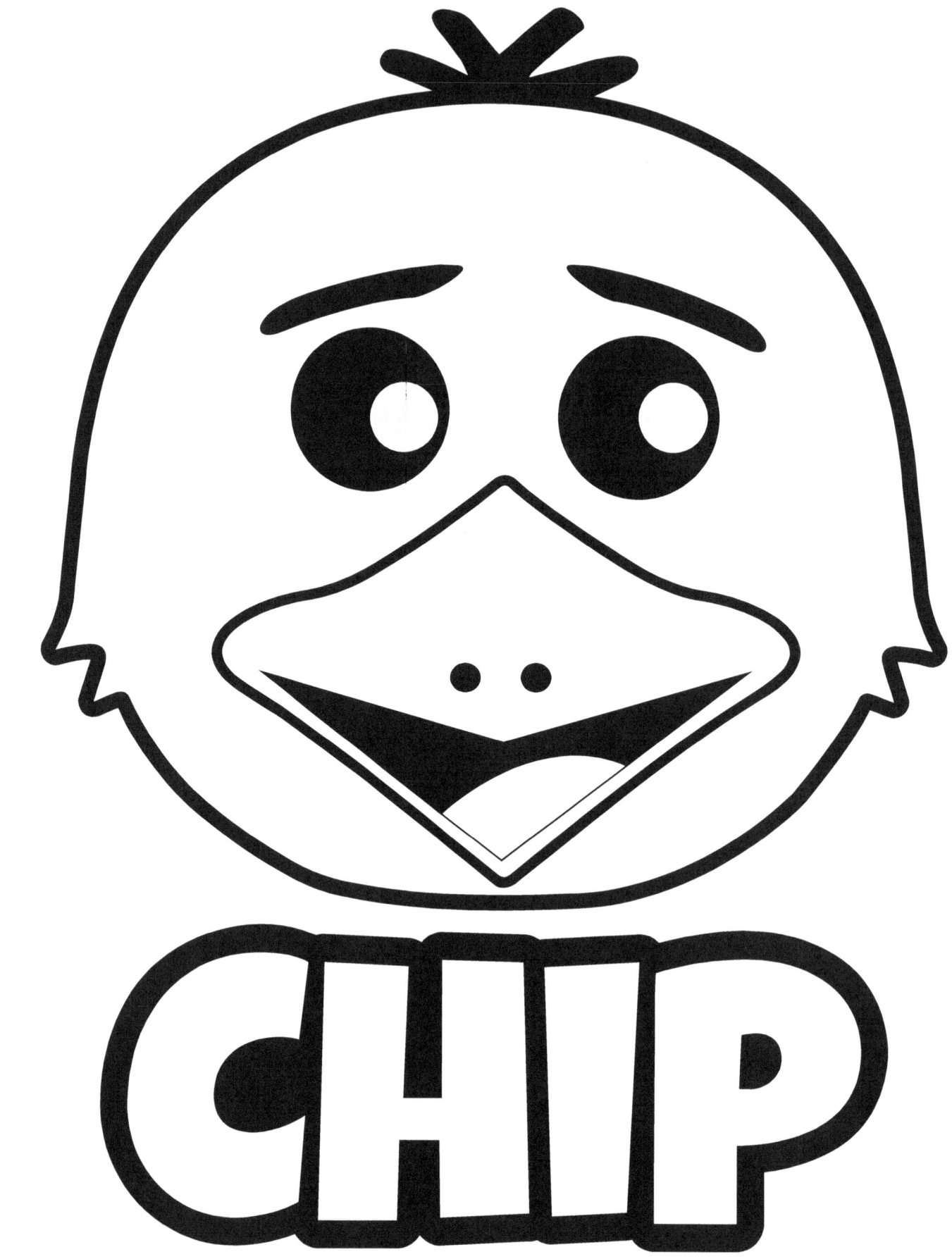

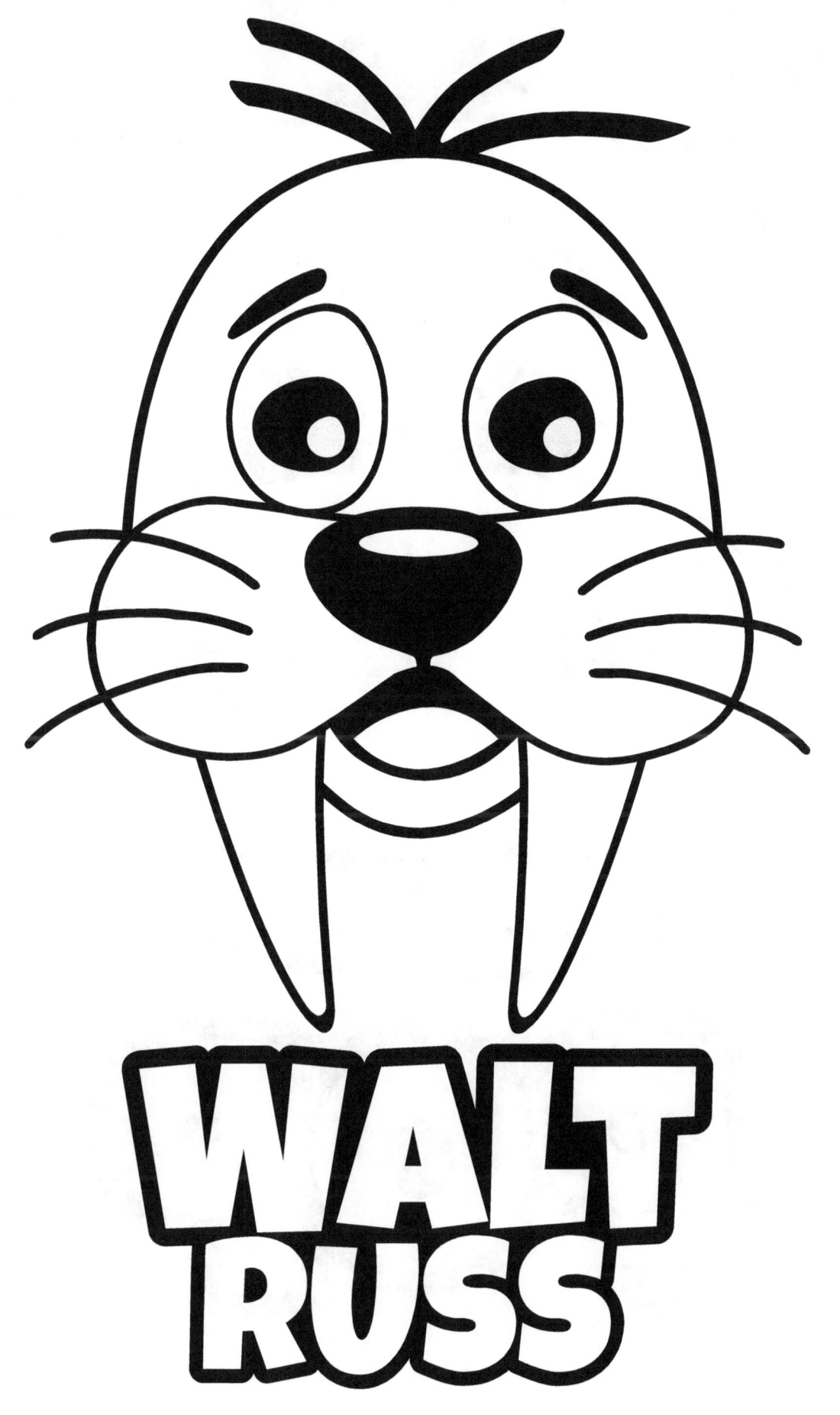

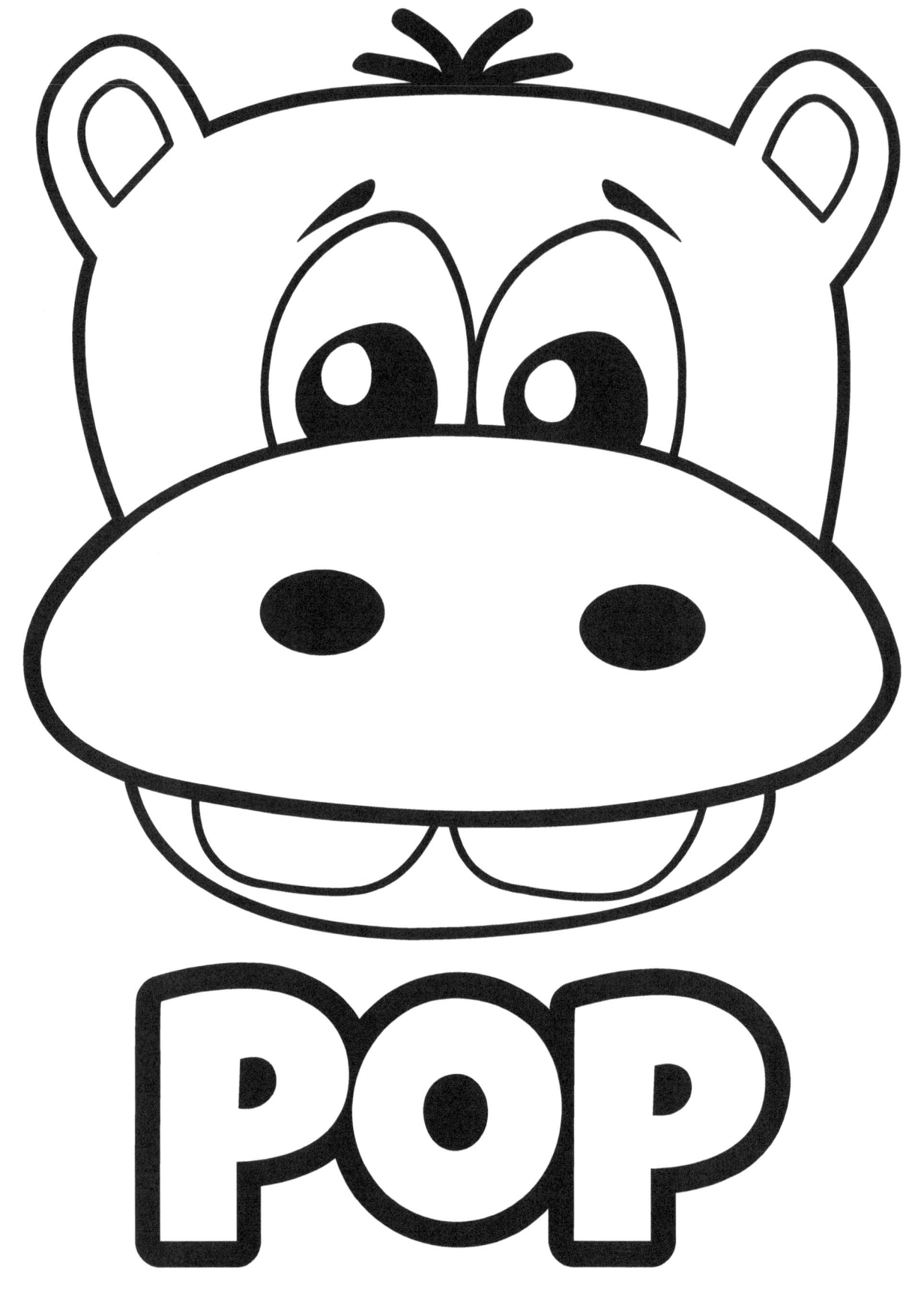

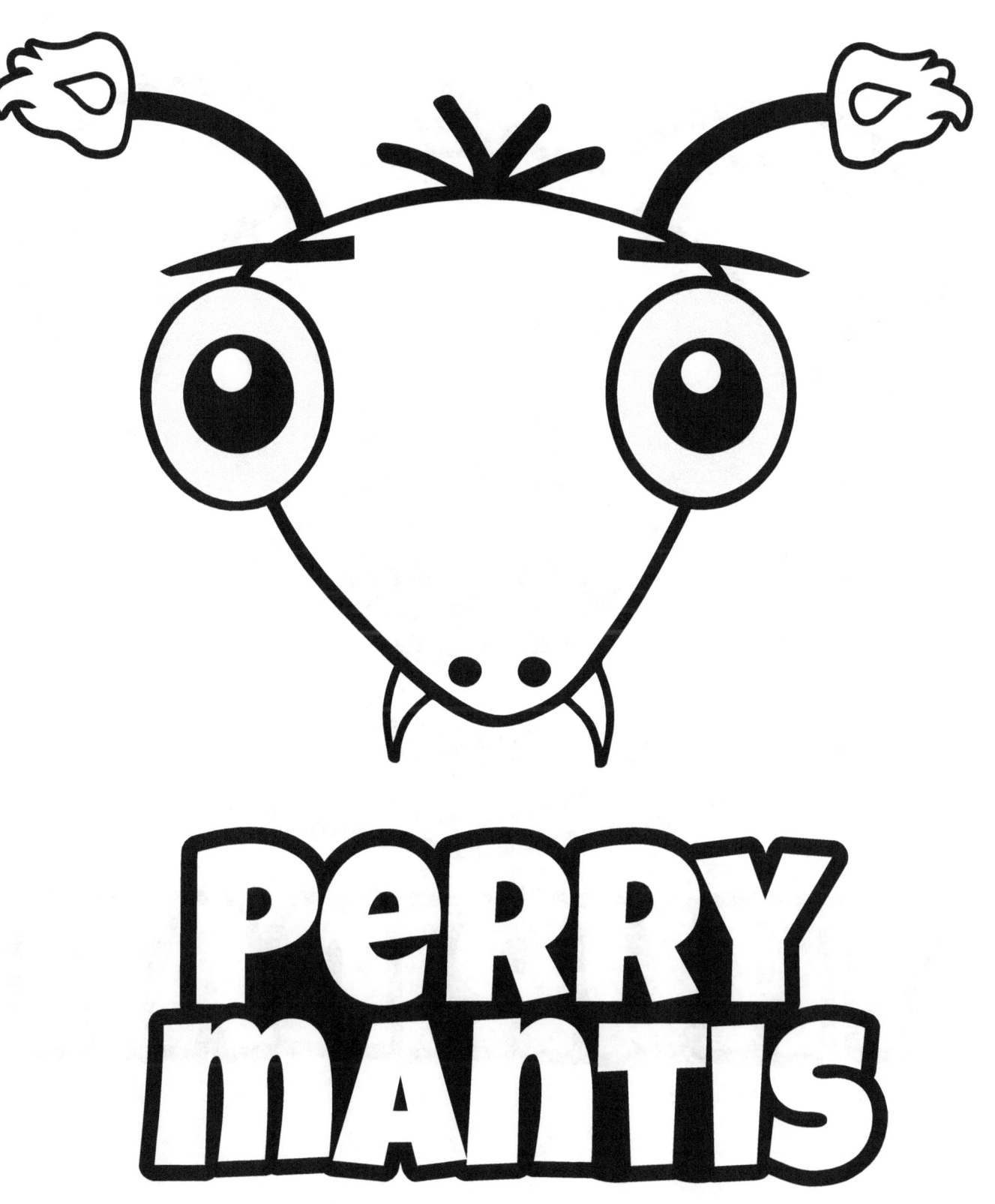

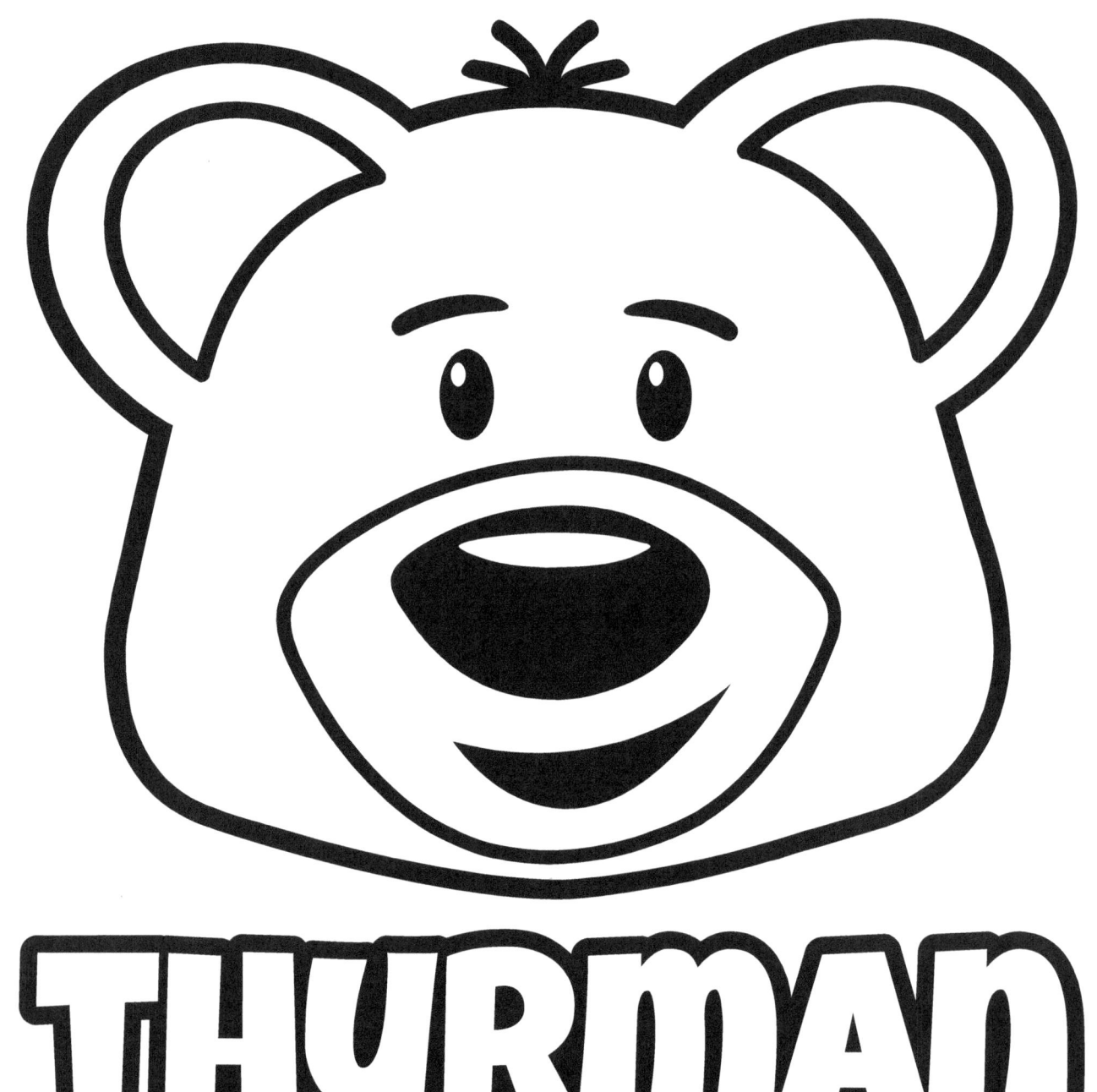

THURMAN

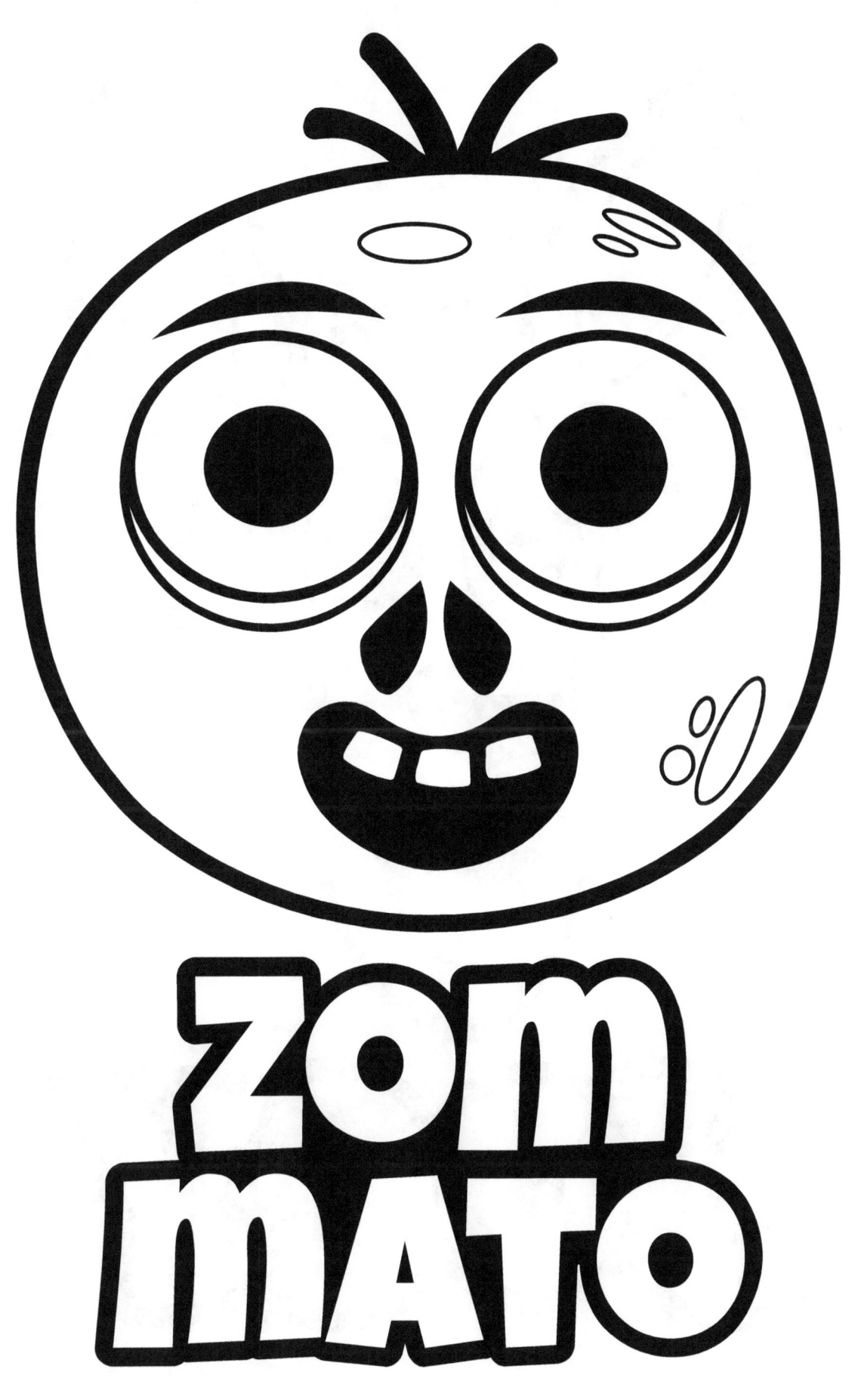

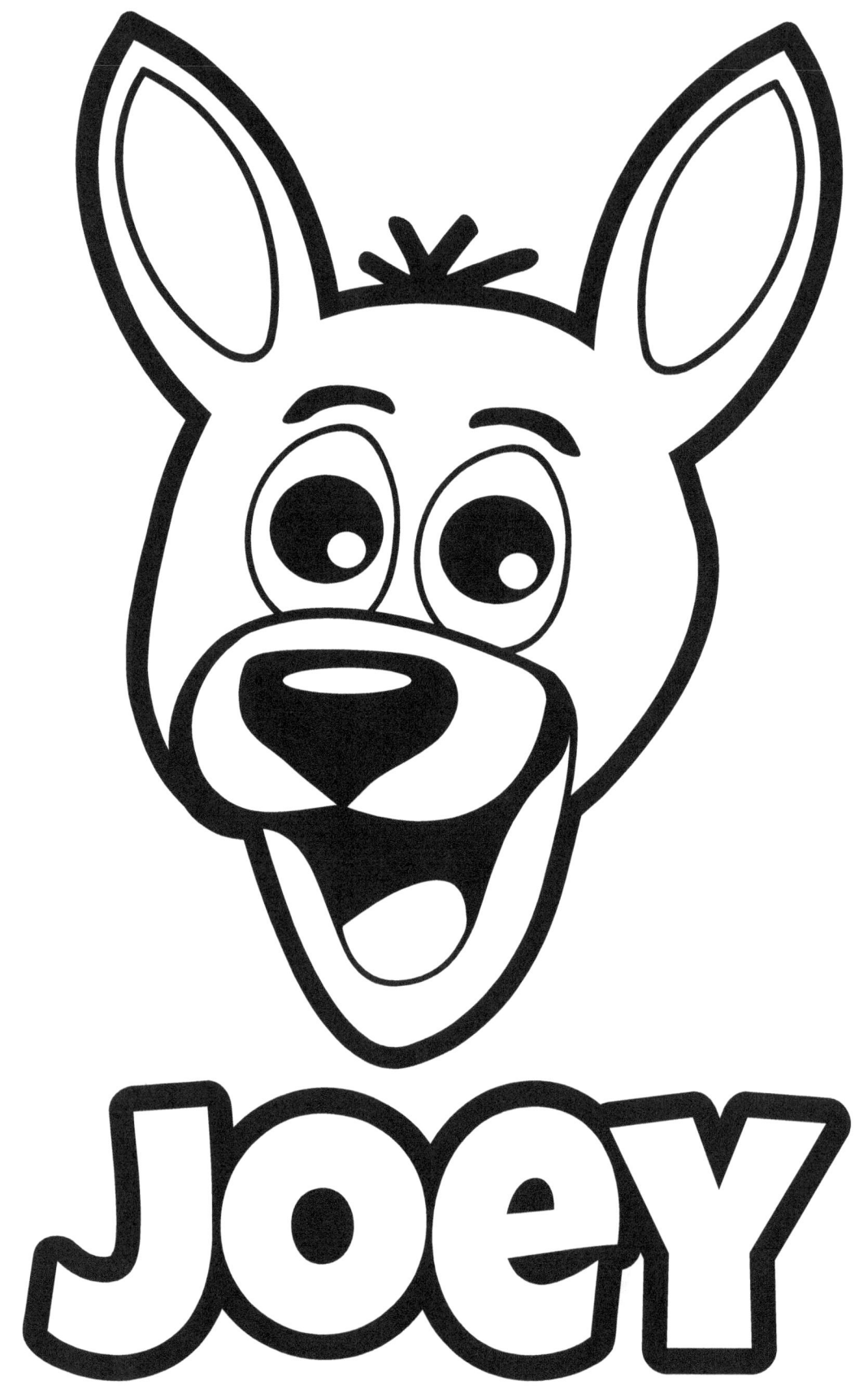

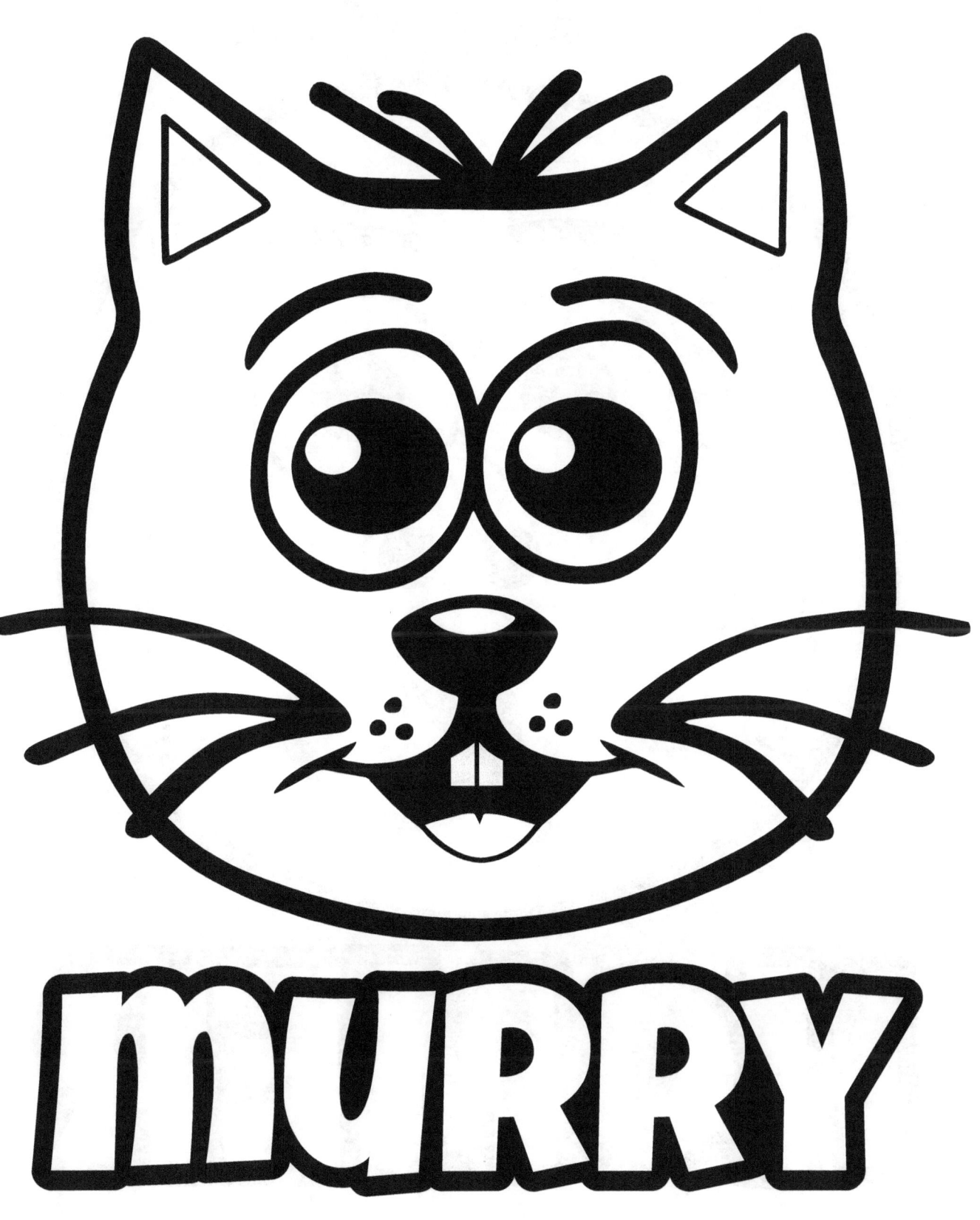

MURRY

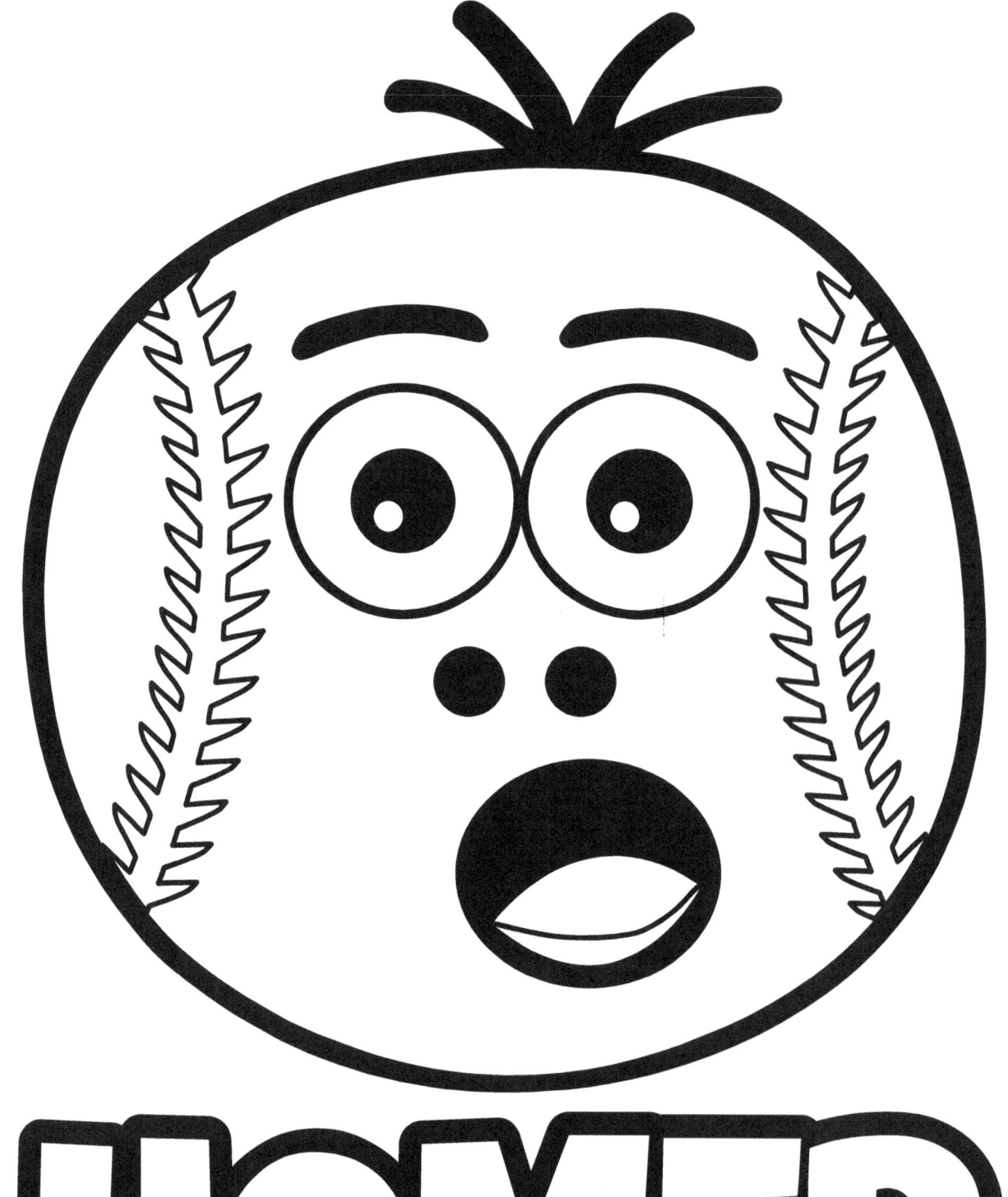

HOMER

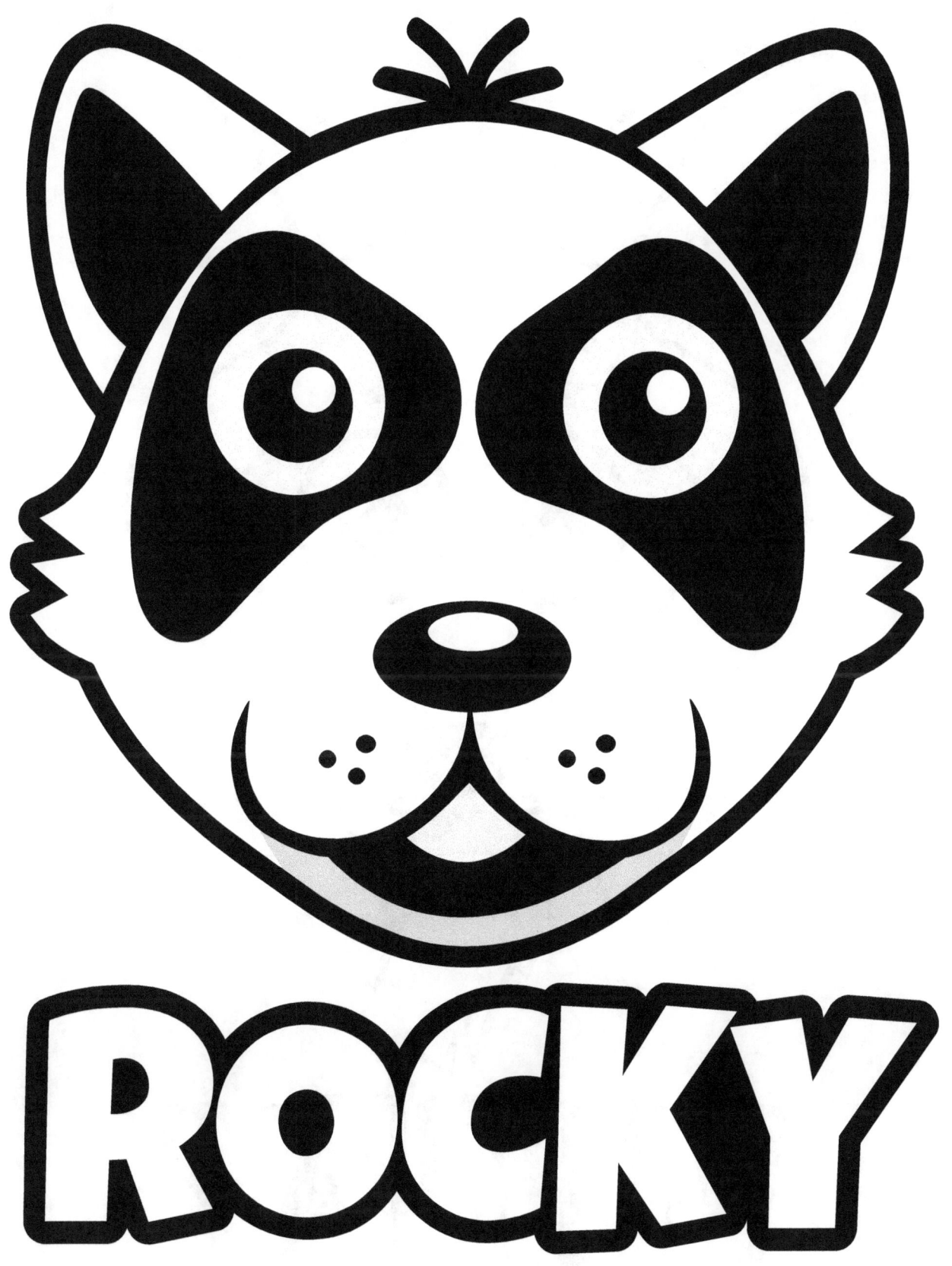

ROCKY

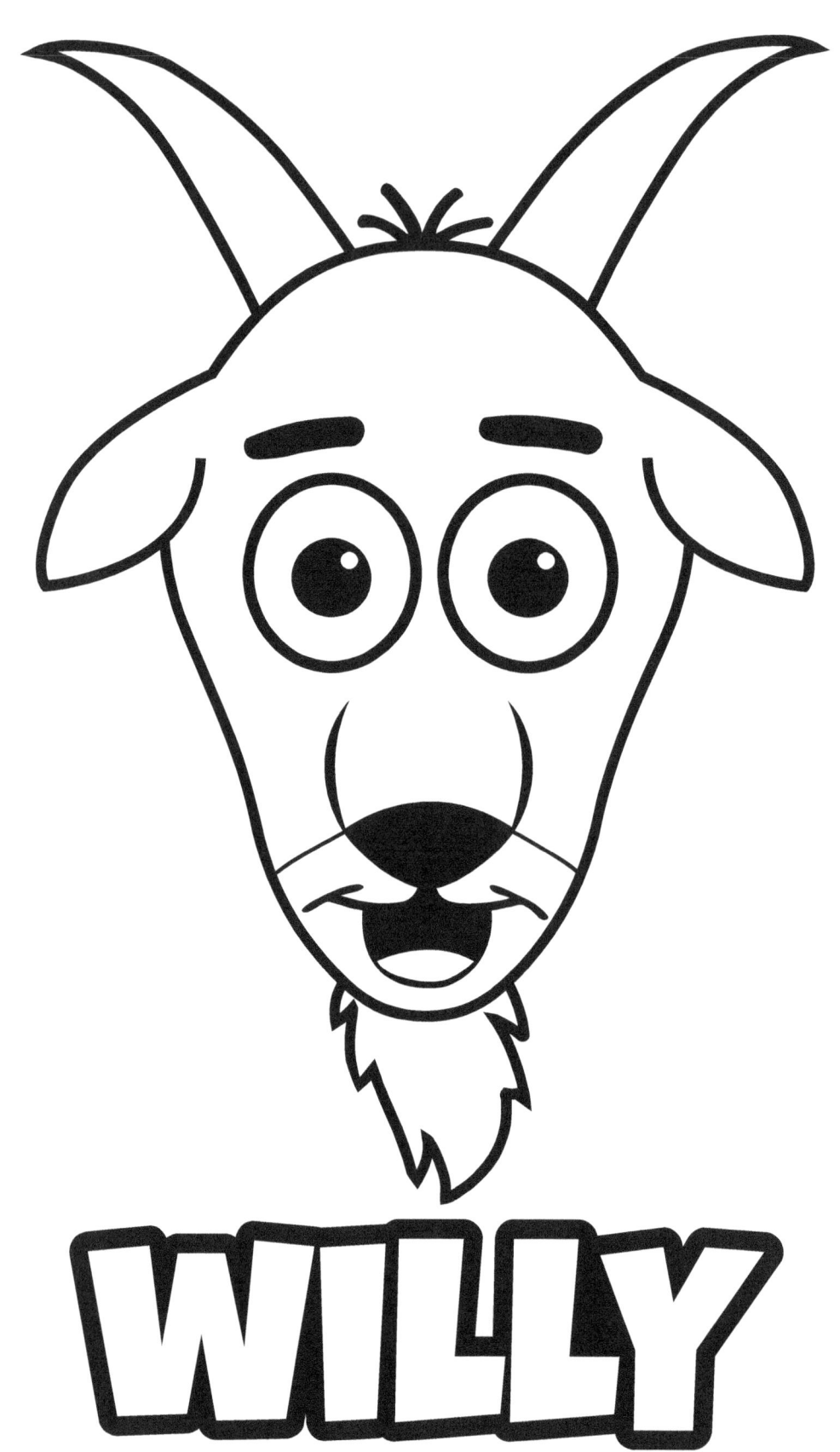

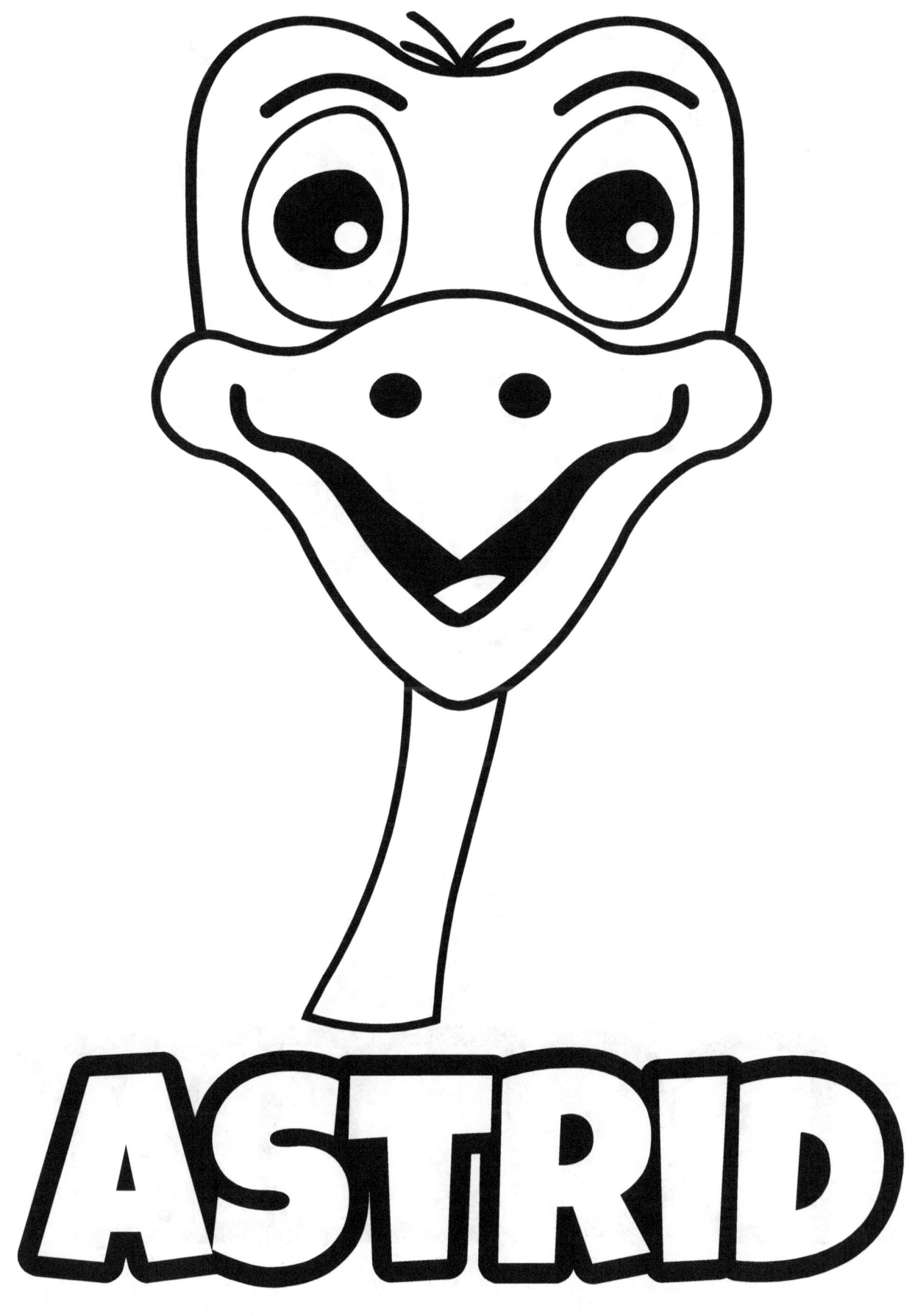

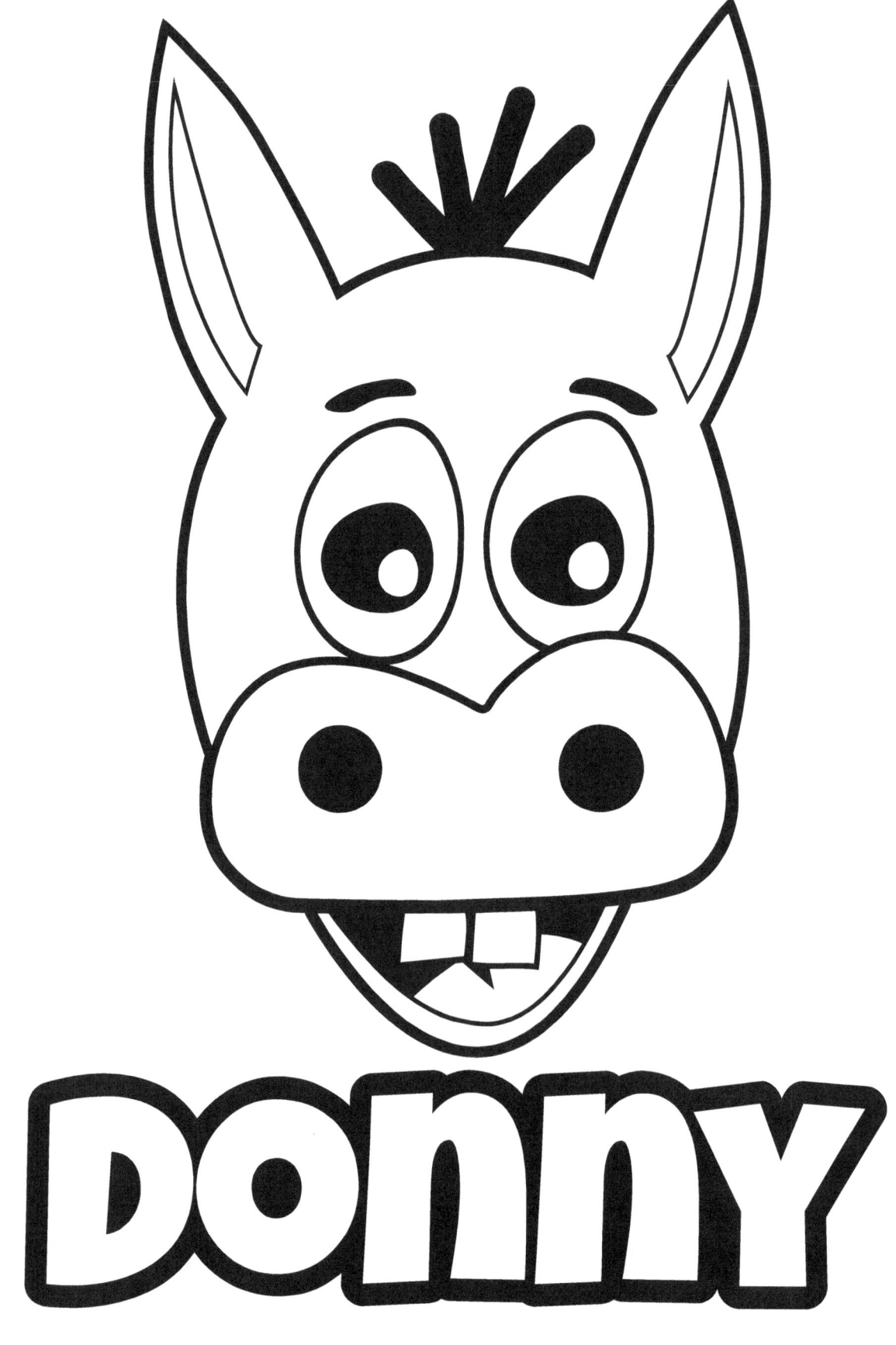

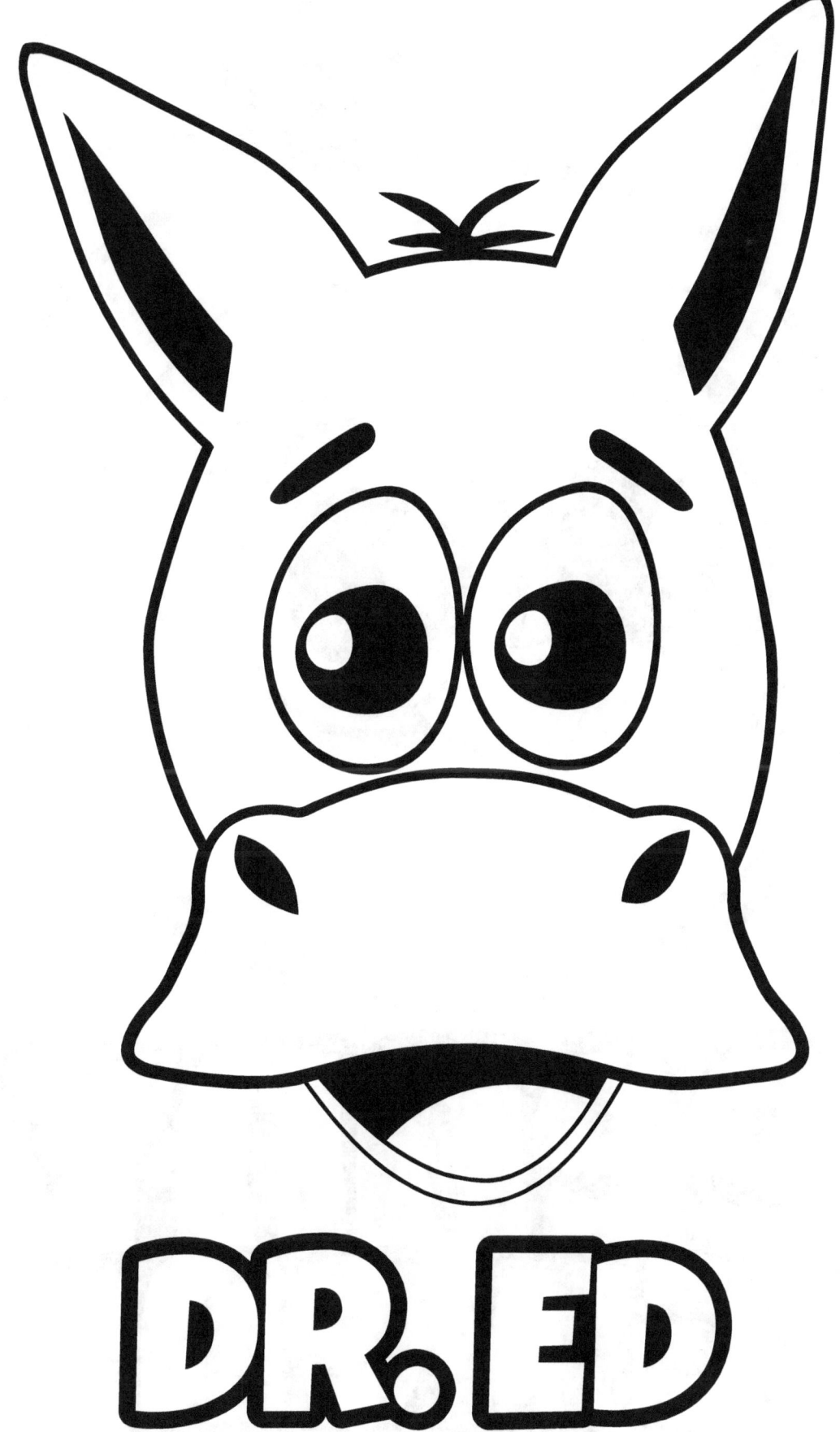

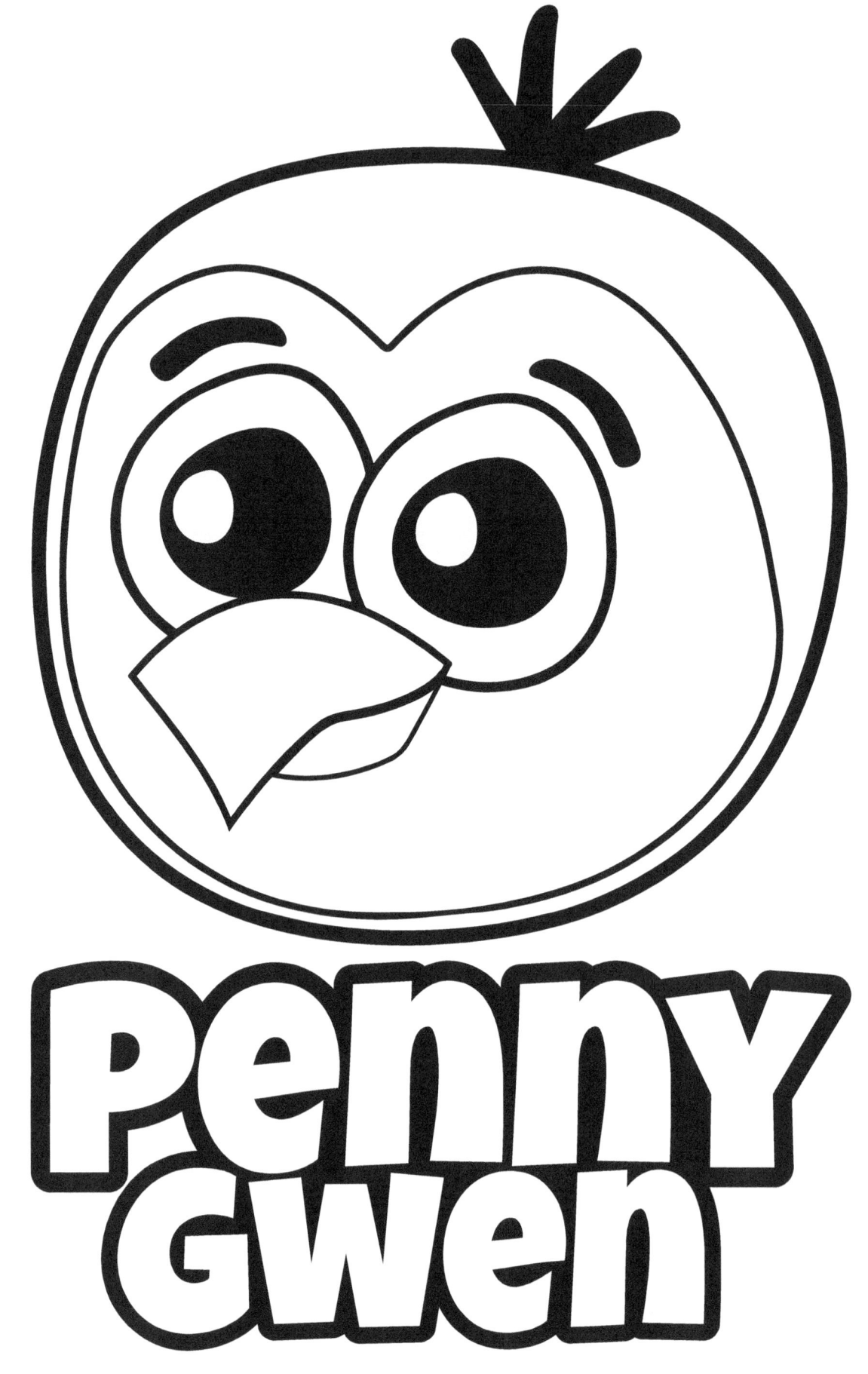

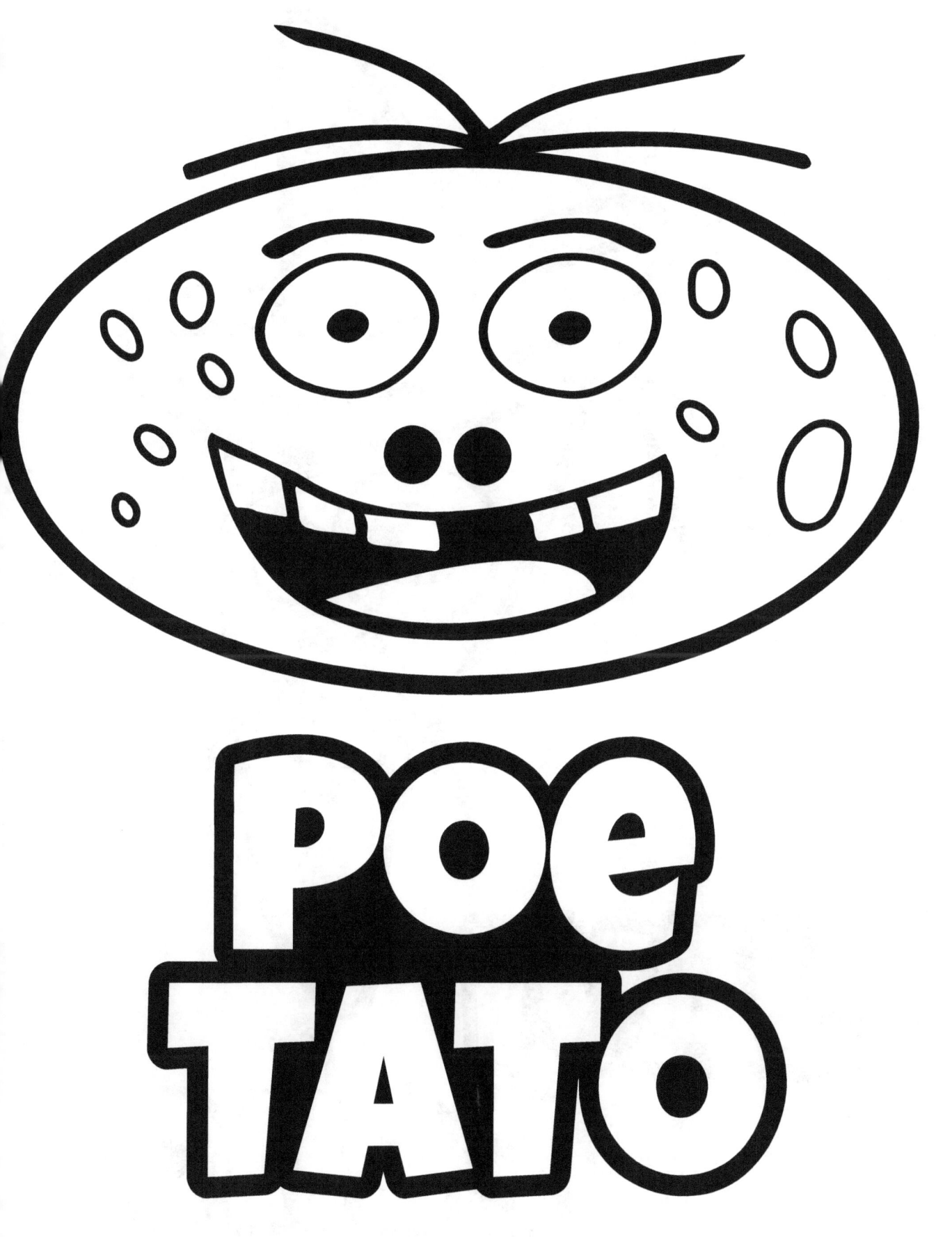

POE TATO

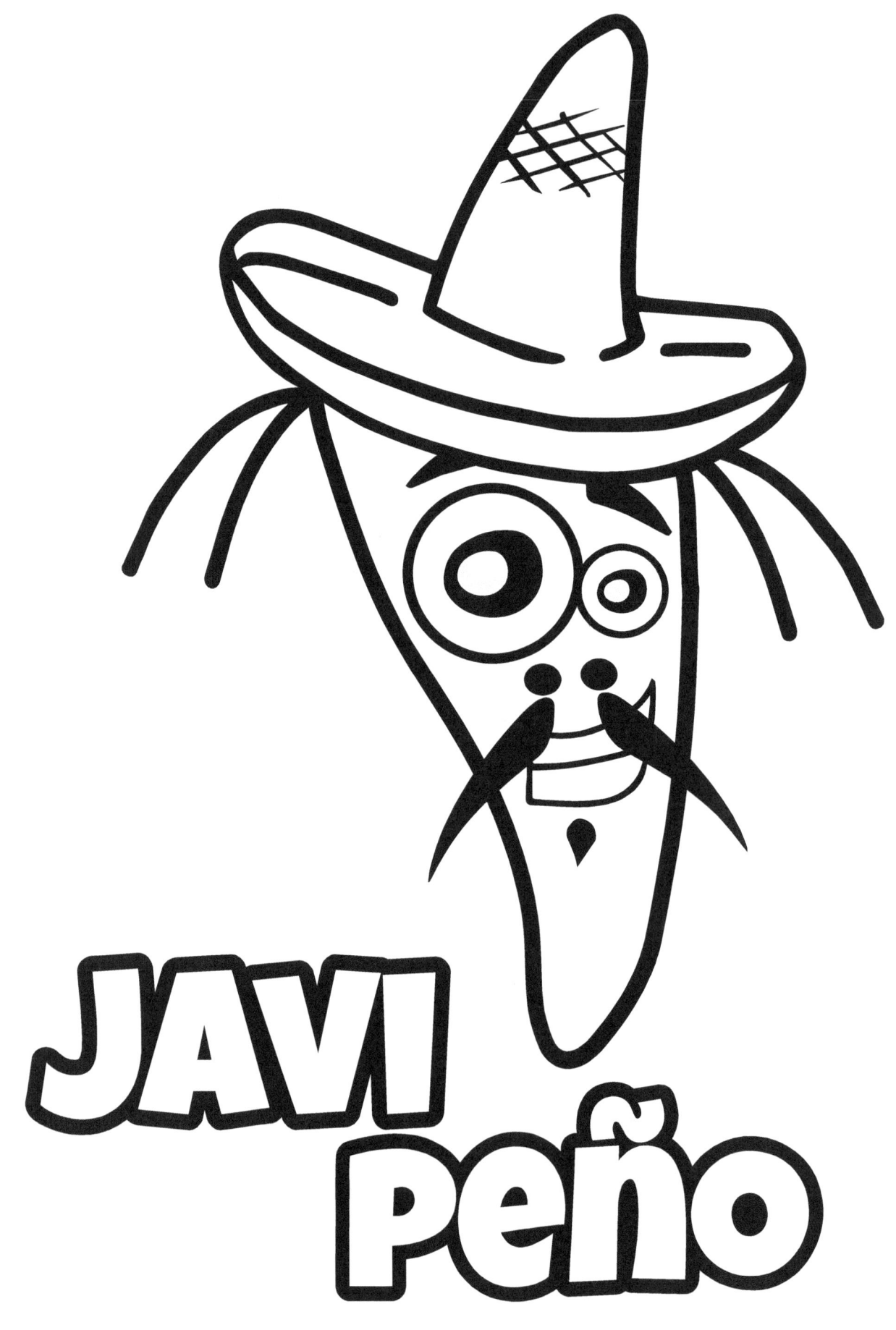

JAVI peño

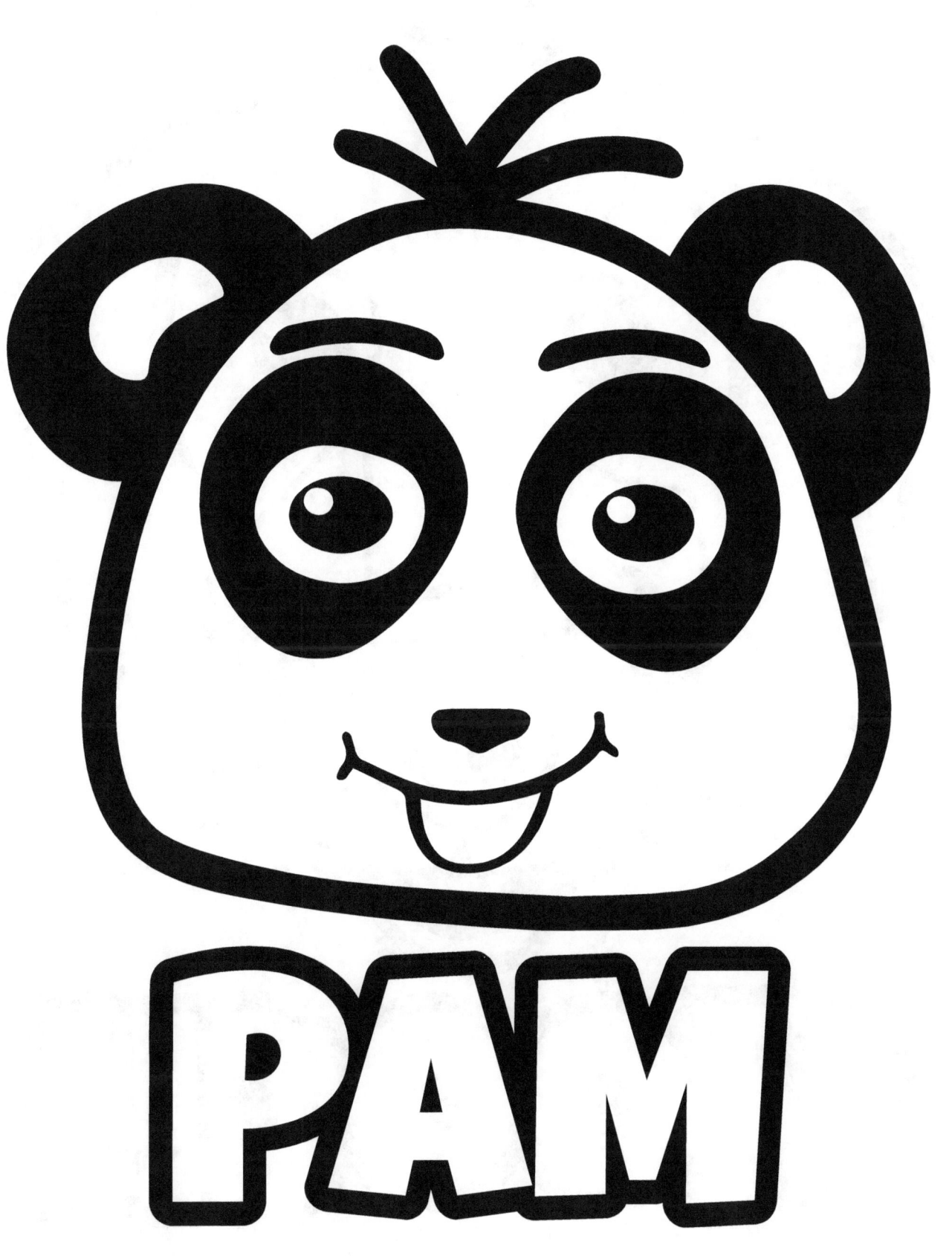

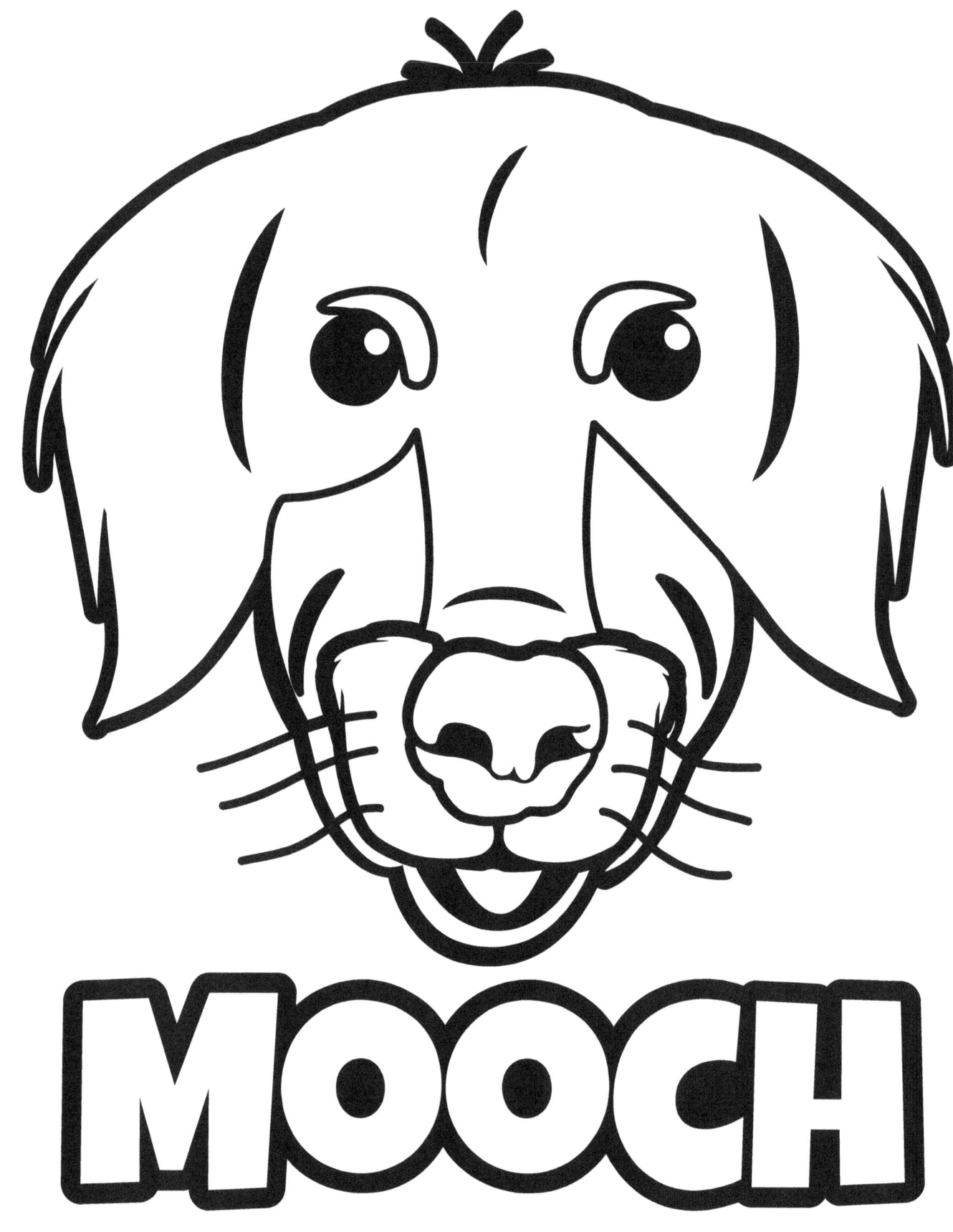

MOOCH

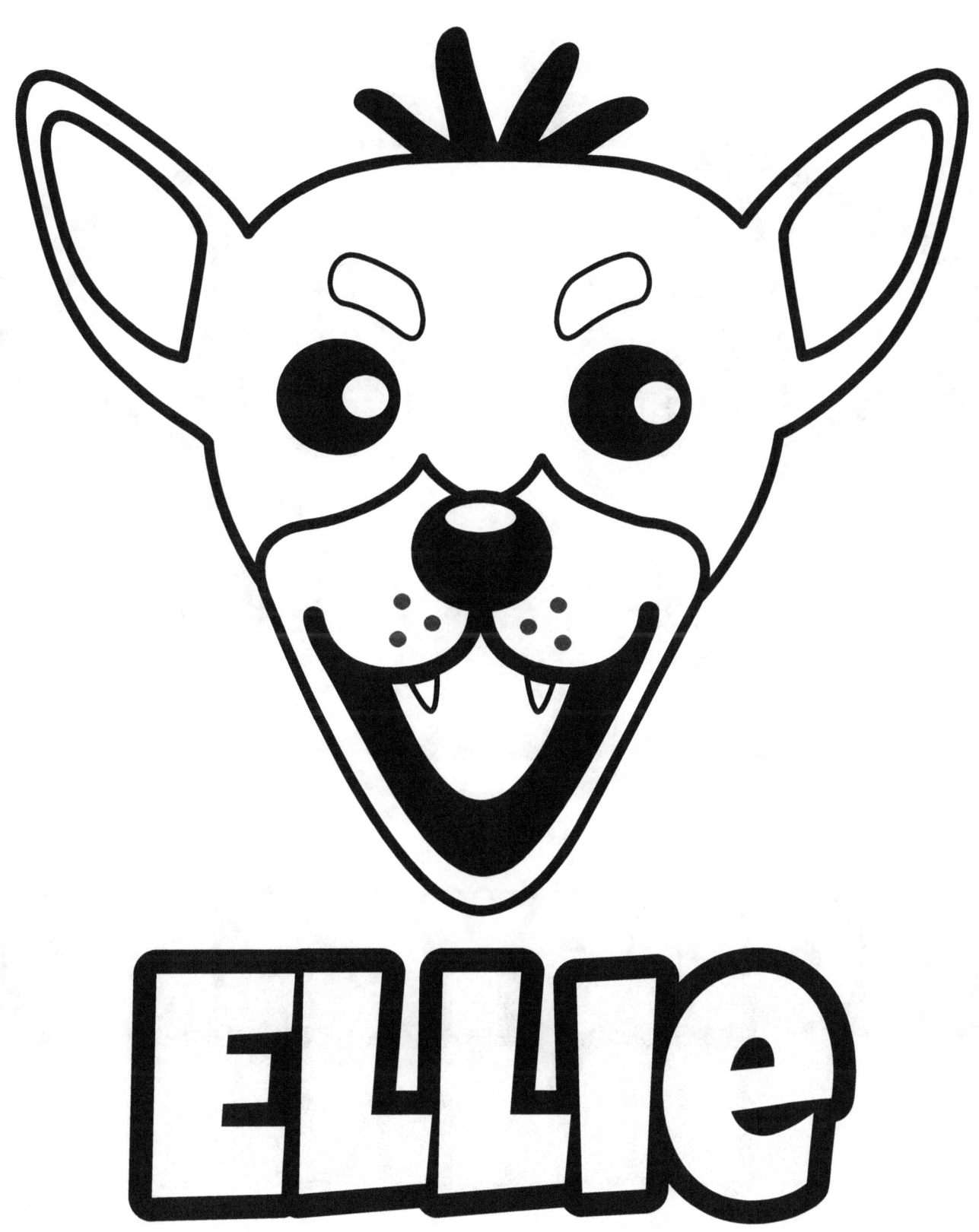

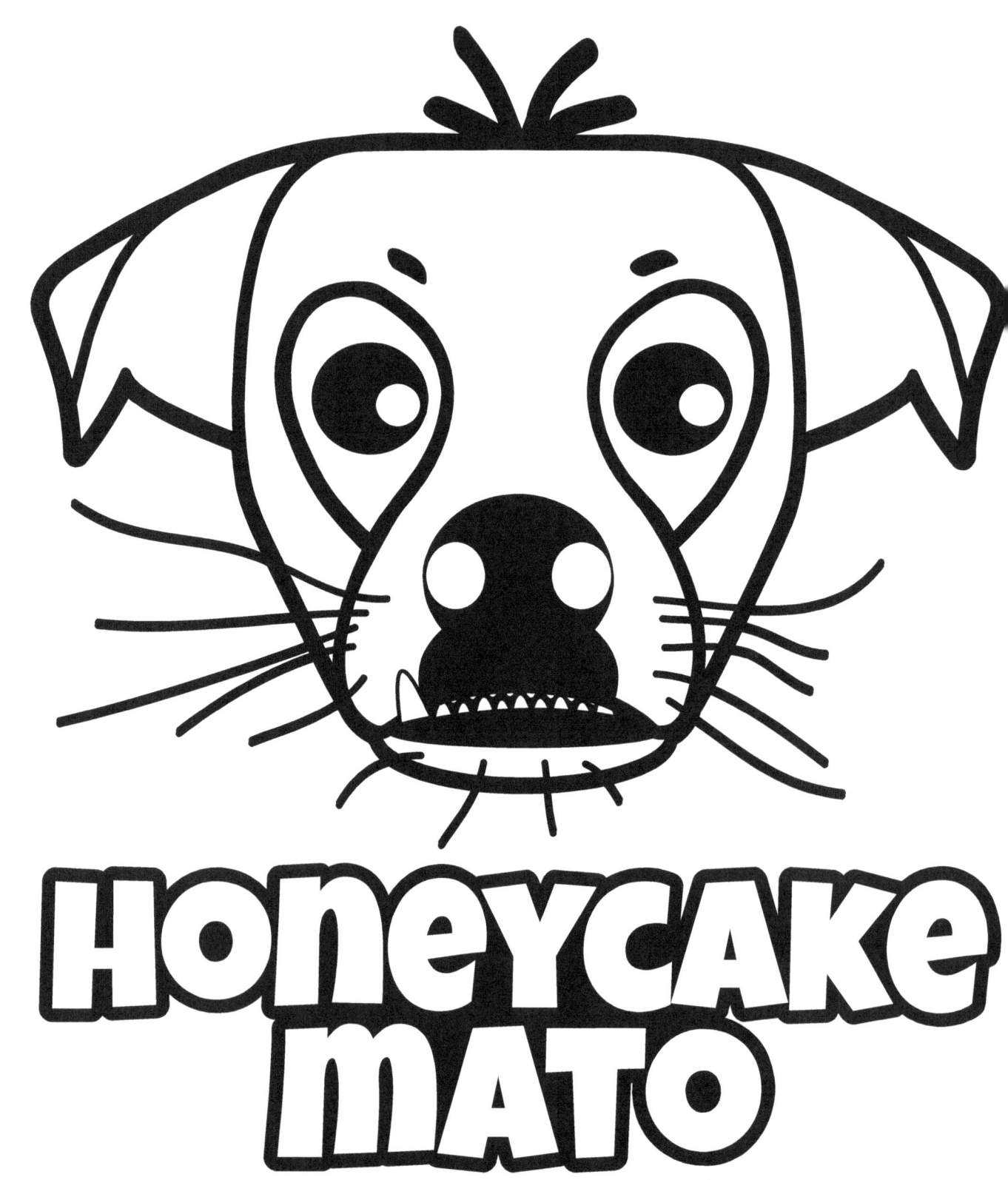

Honeycake Mato

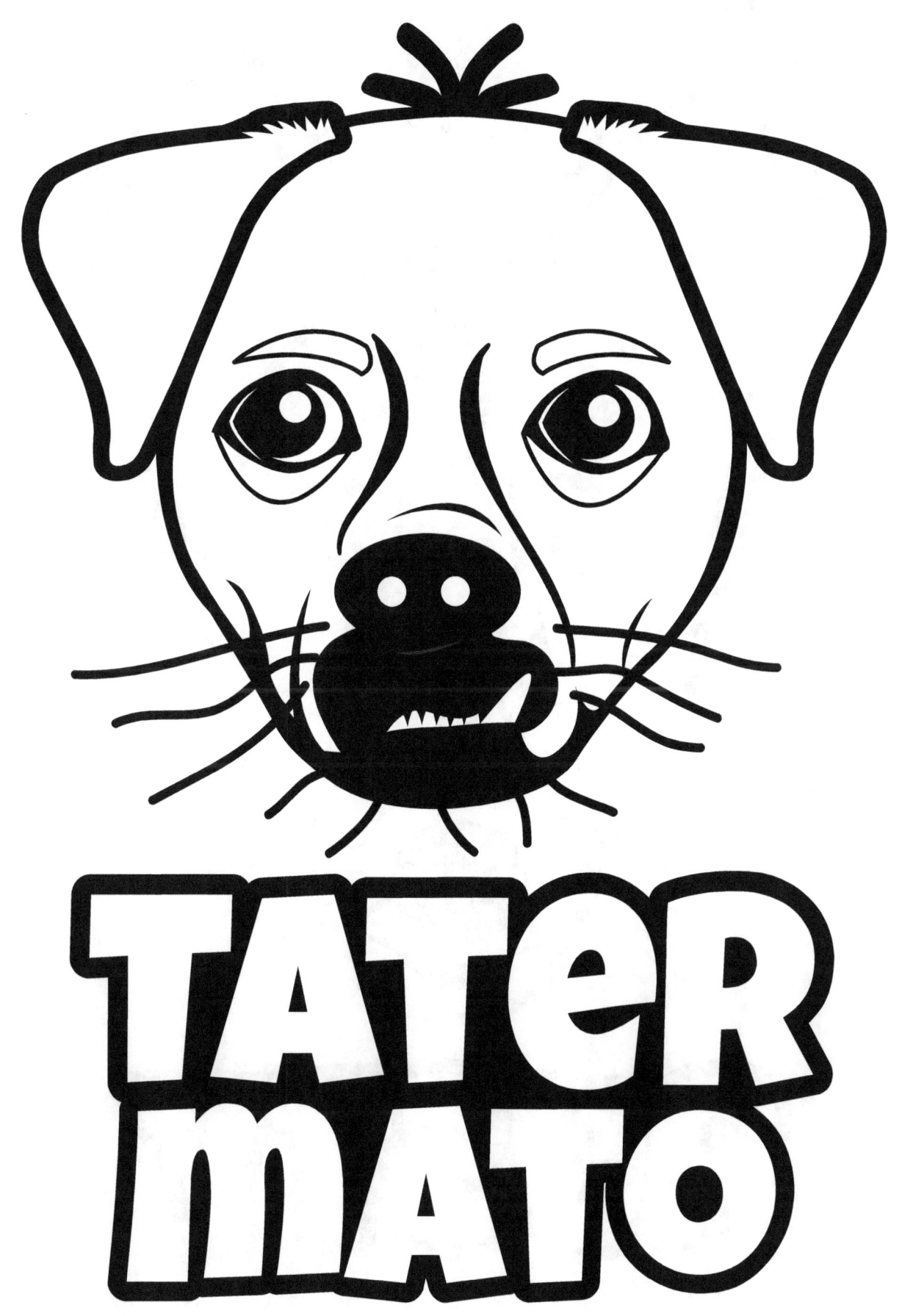

TATER
MATO

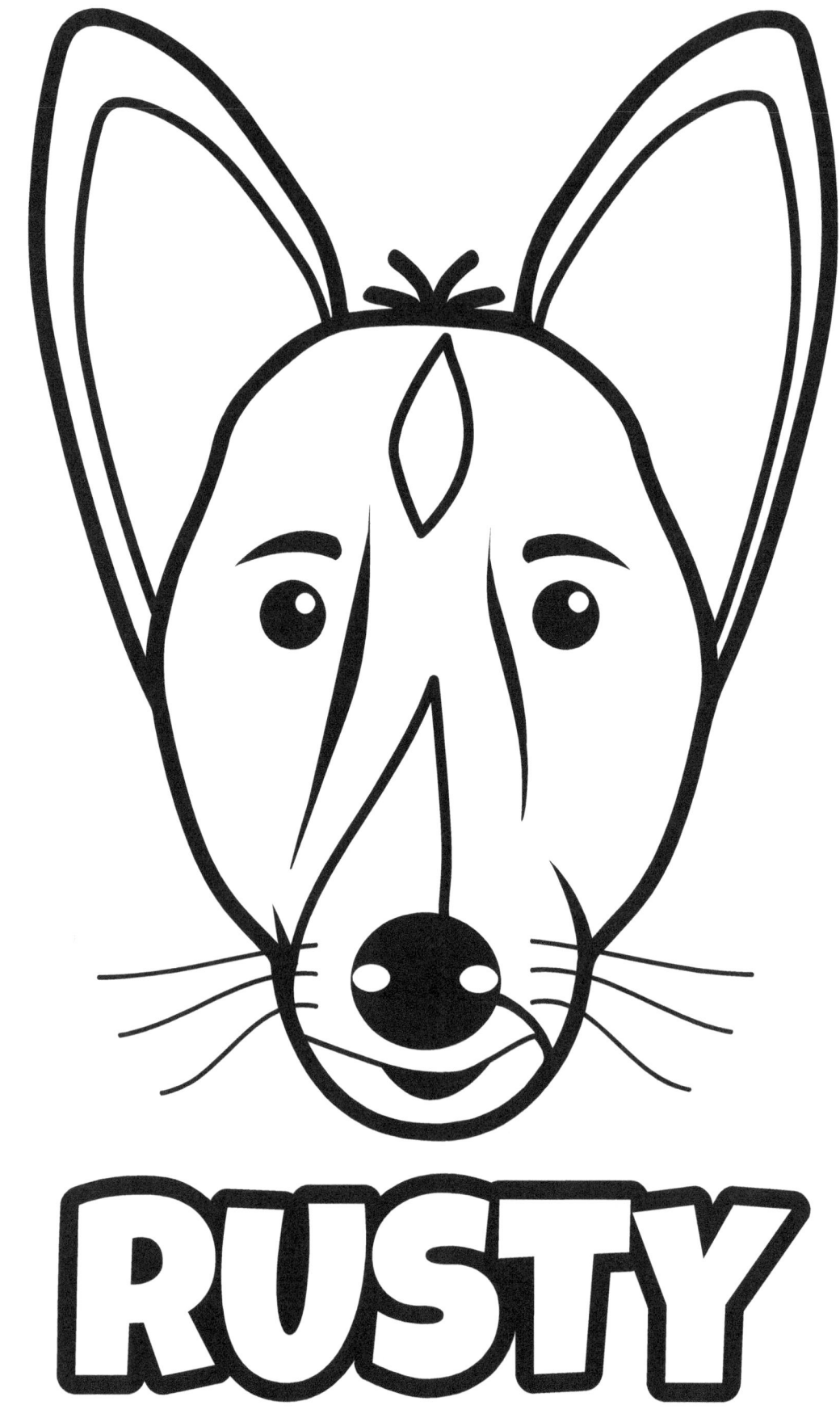

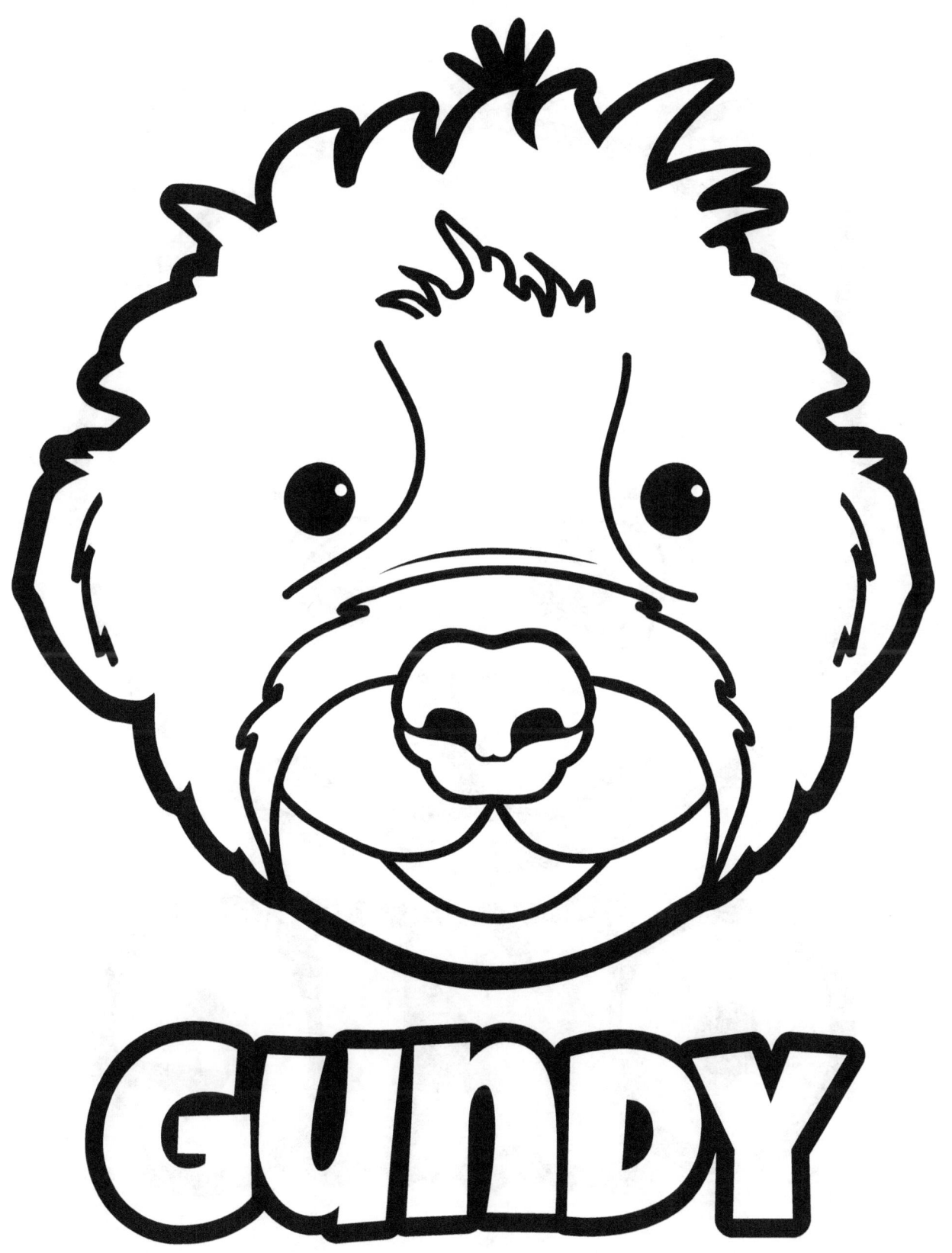

GUNDY

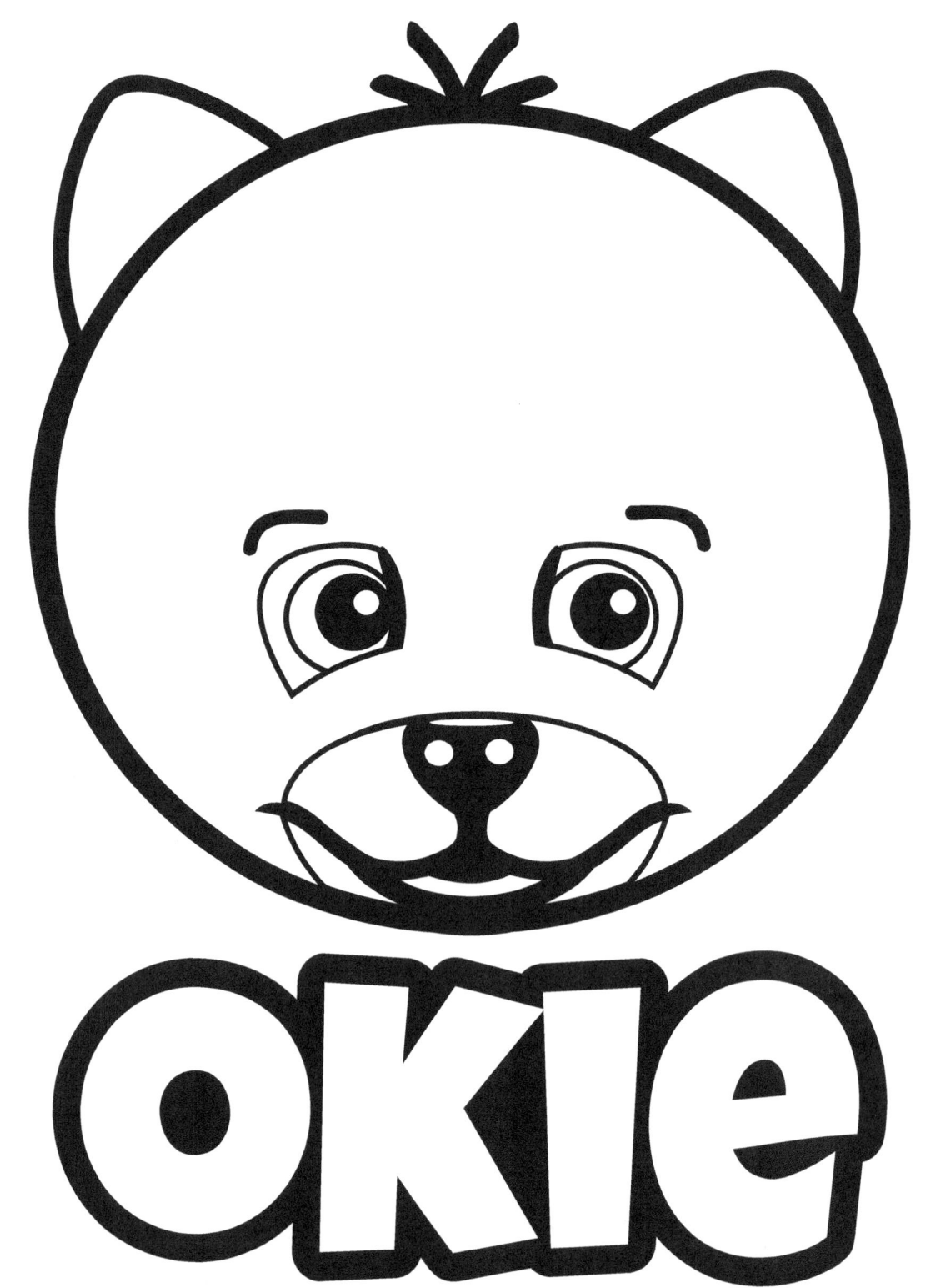

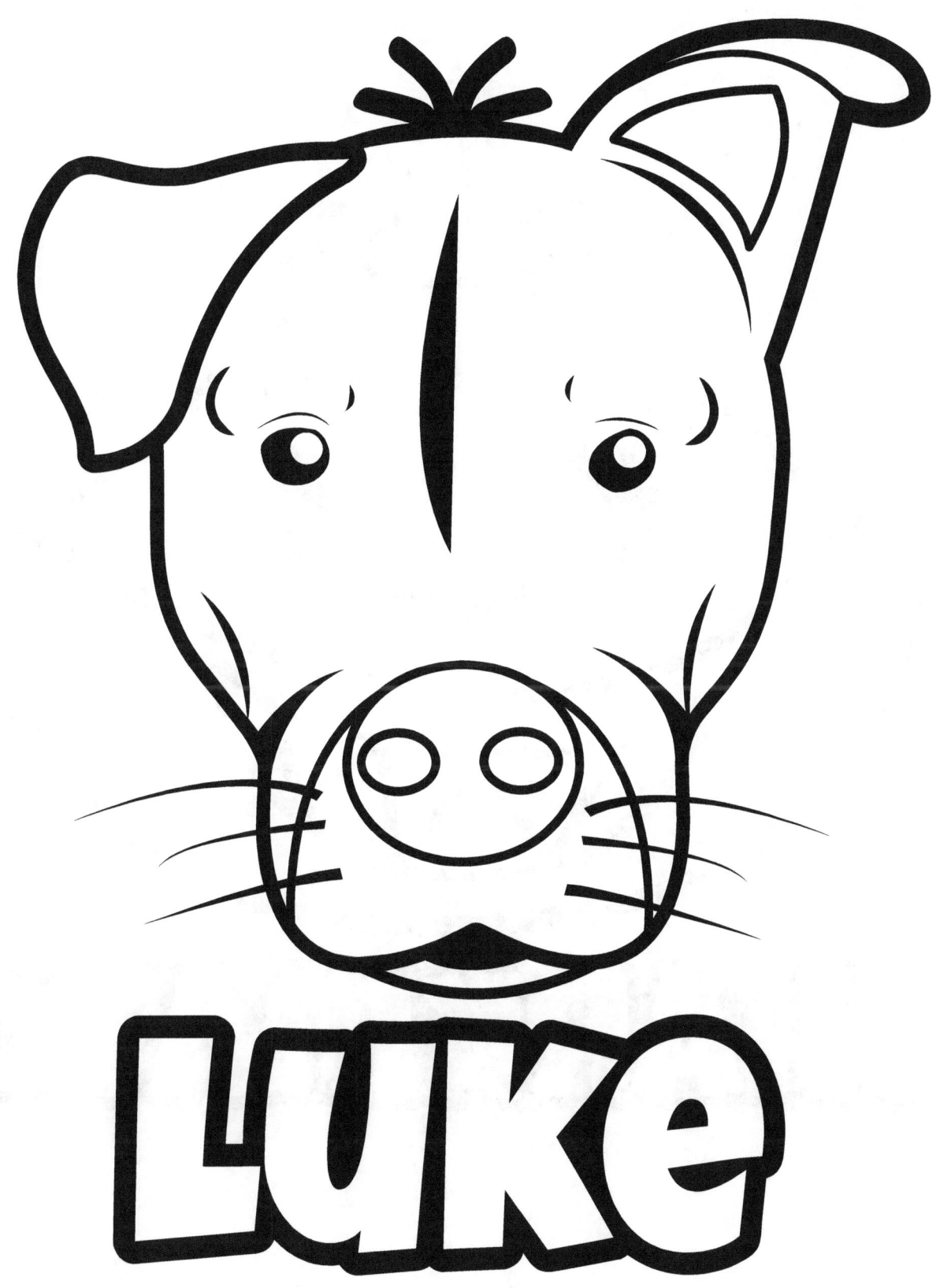

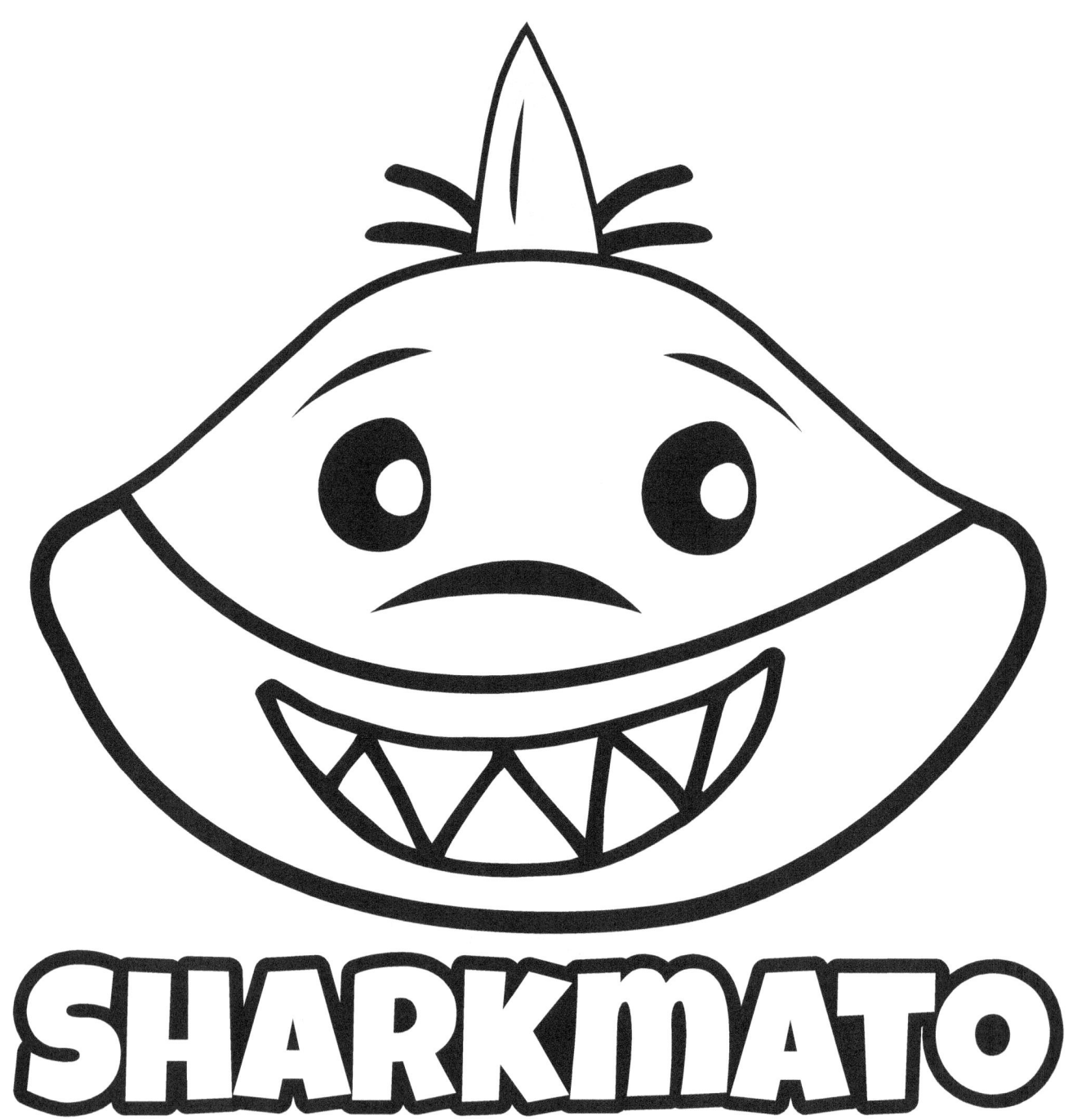

SHARKMATO

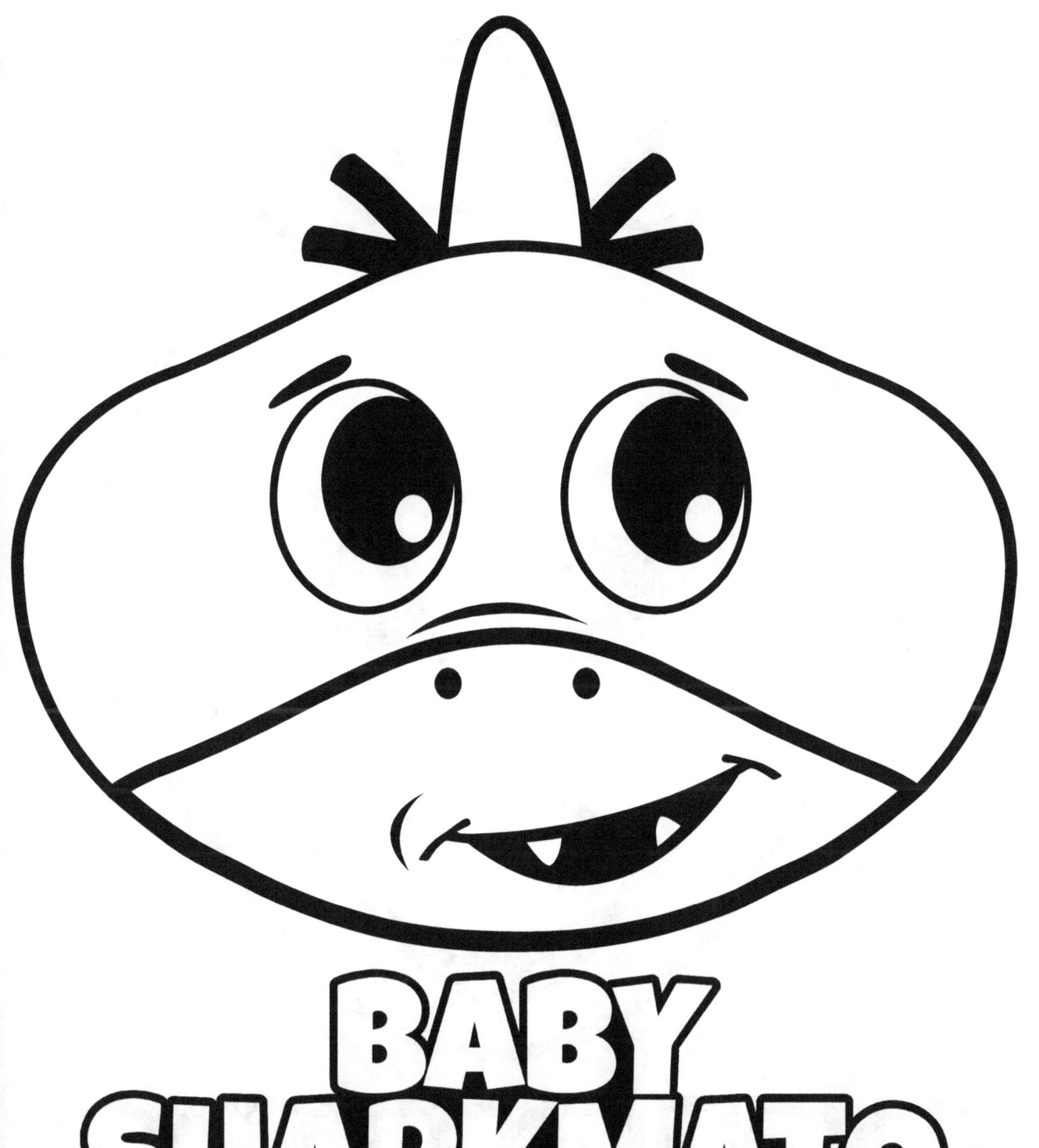

BABY
SHARKMATO

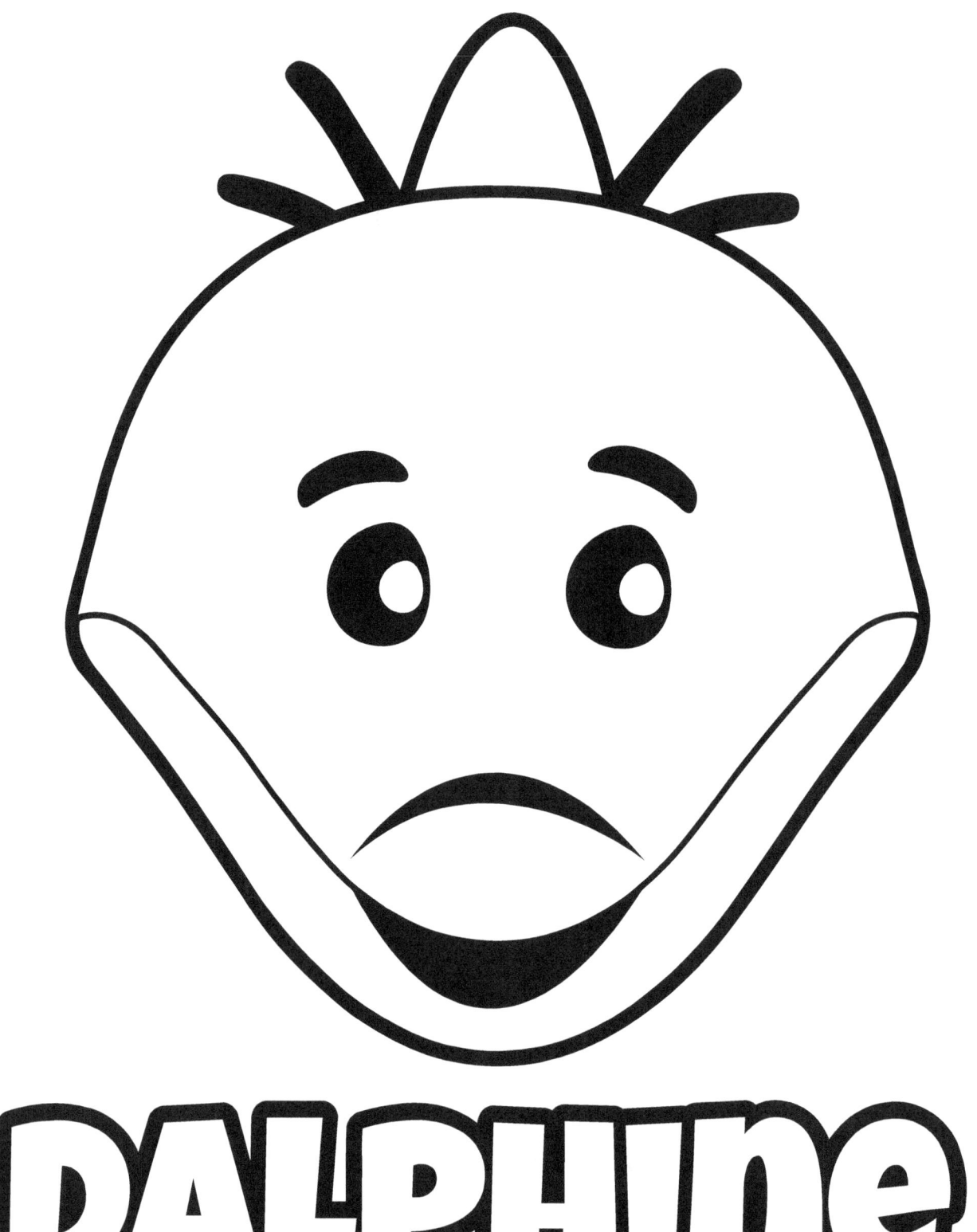

DALPHINE

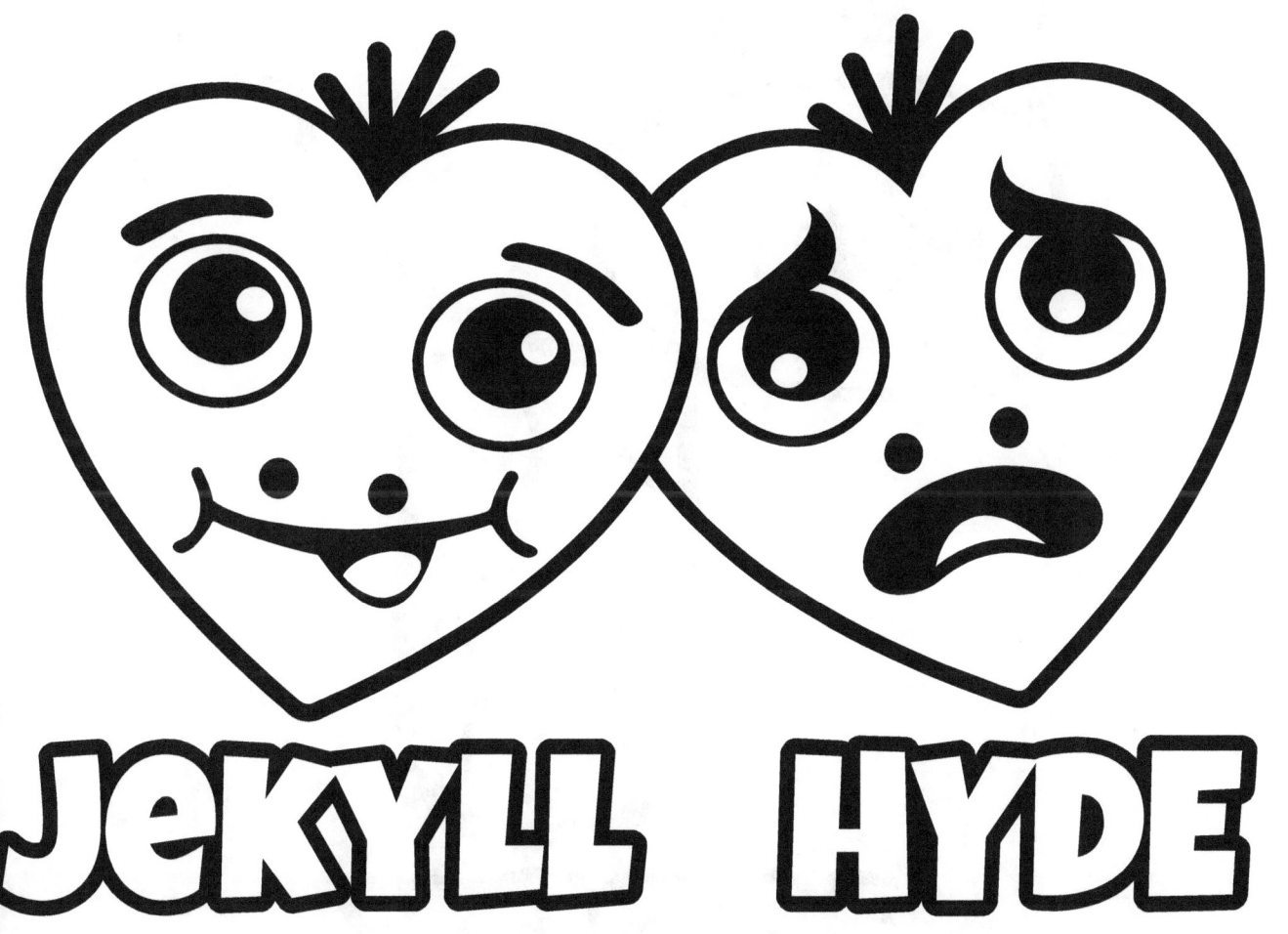

JEKYLL   HYDE

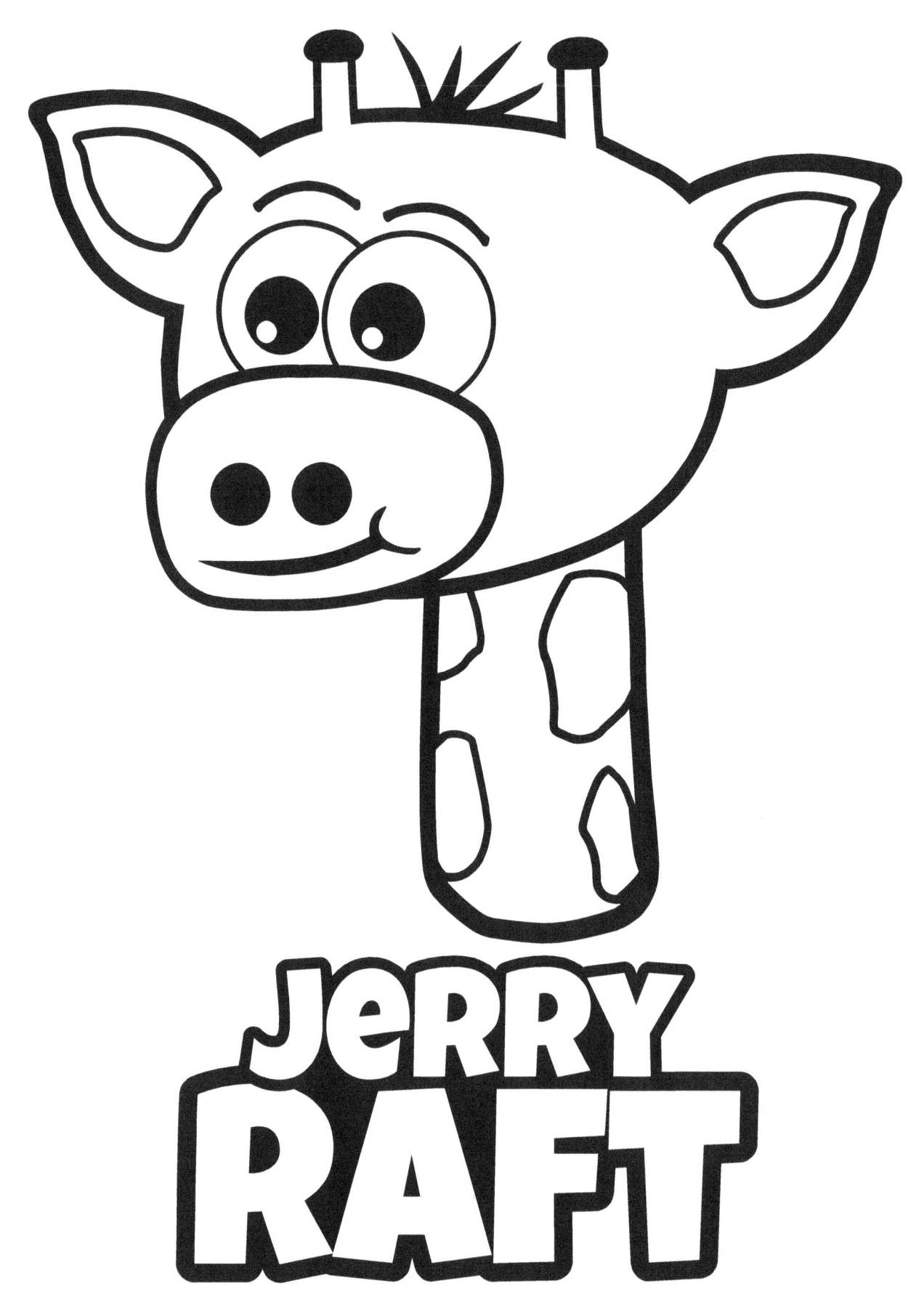

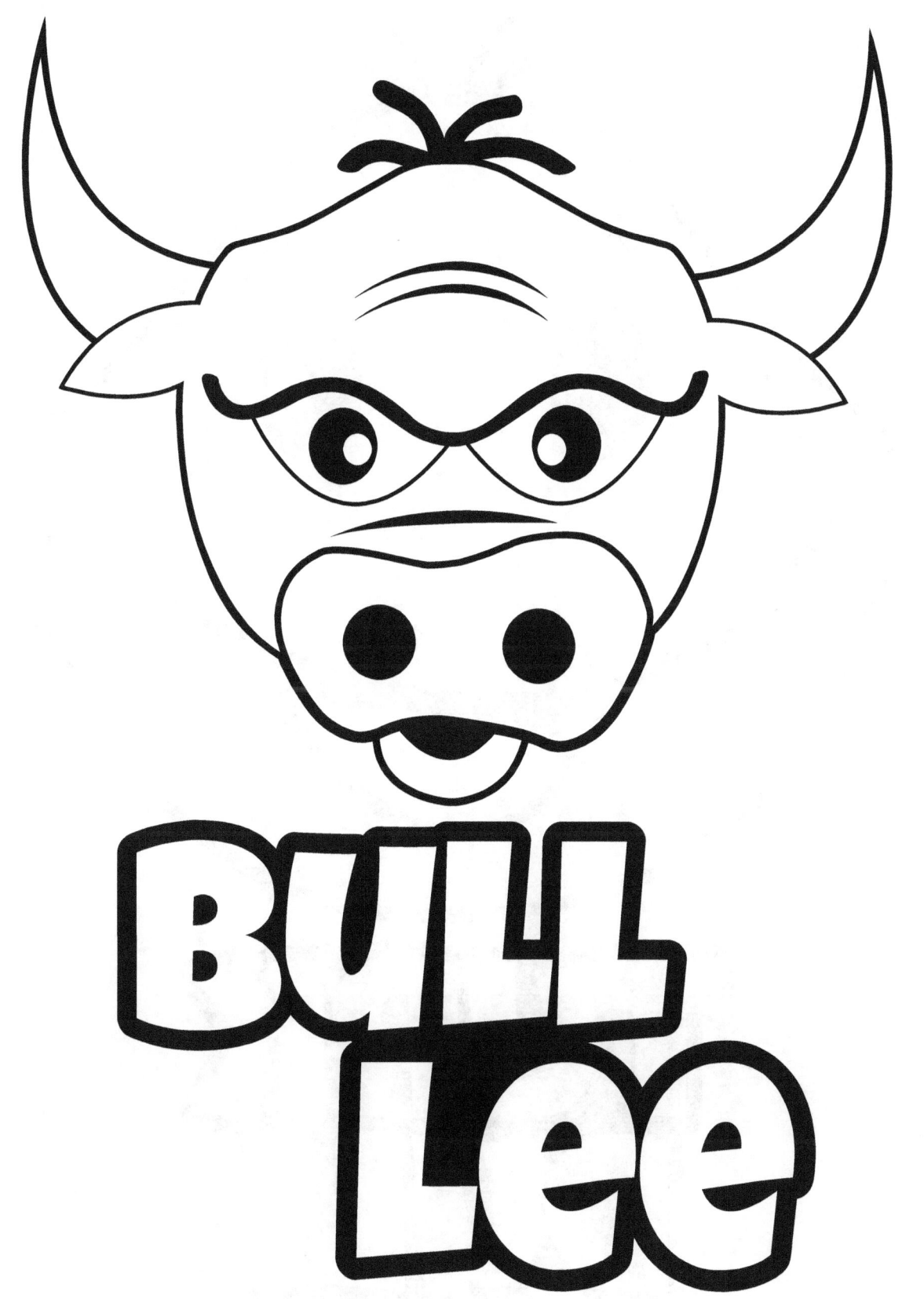

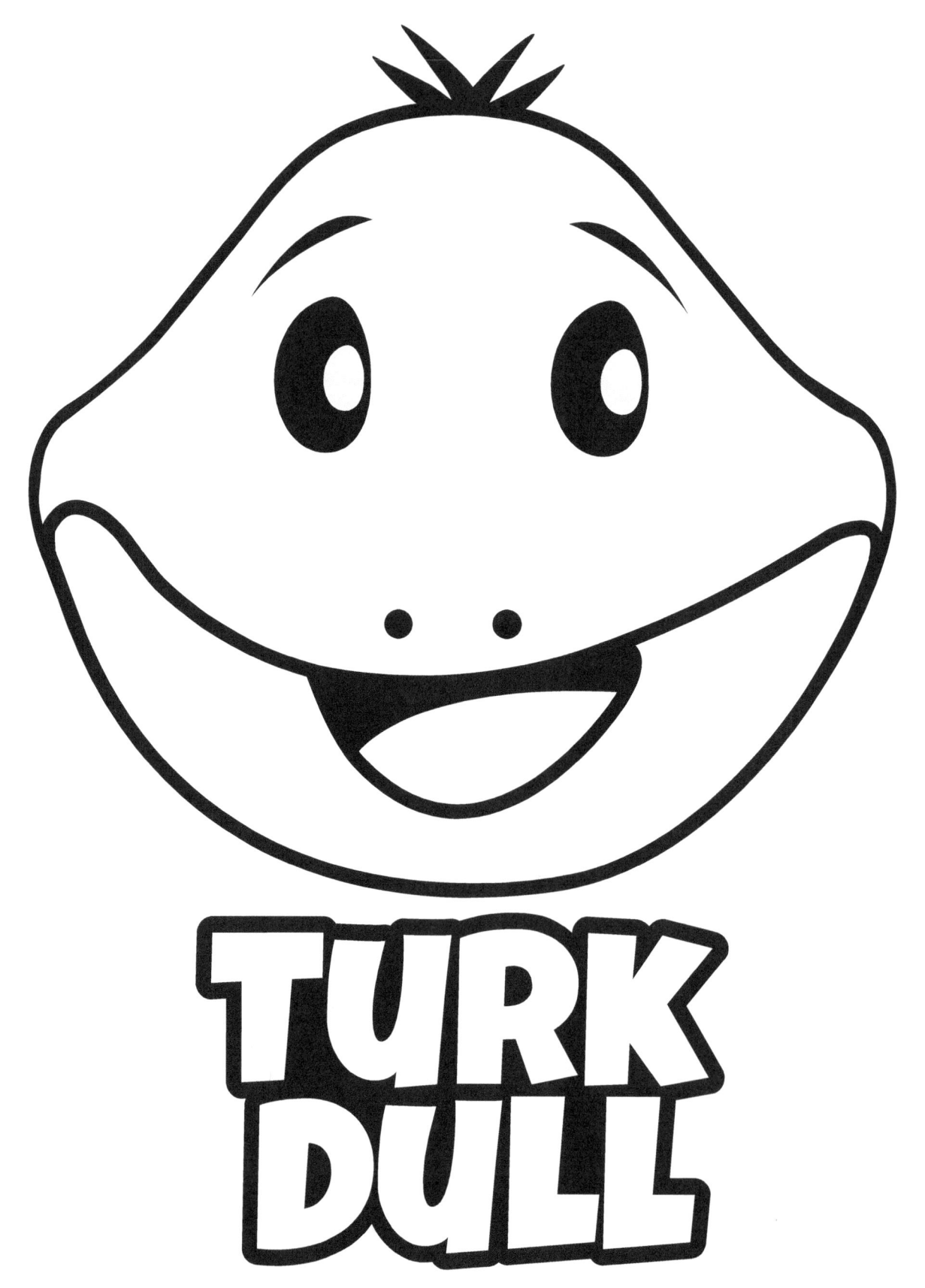

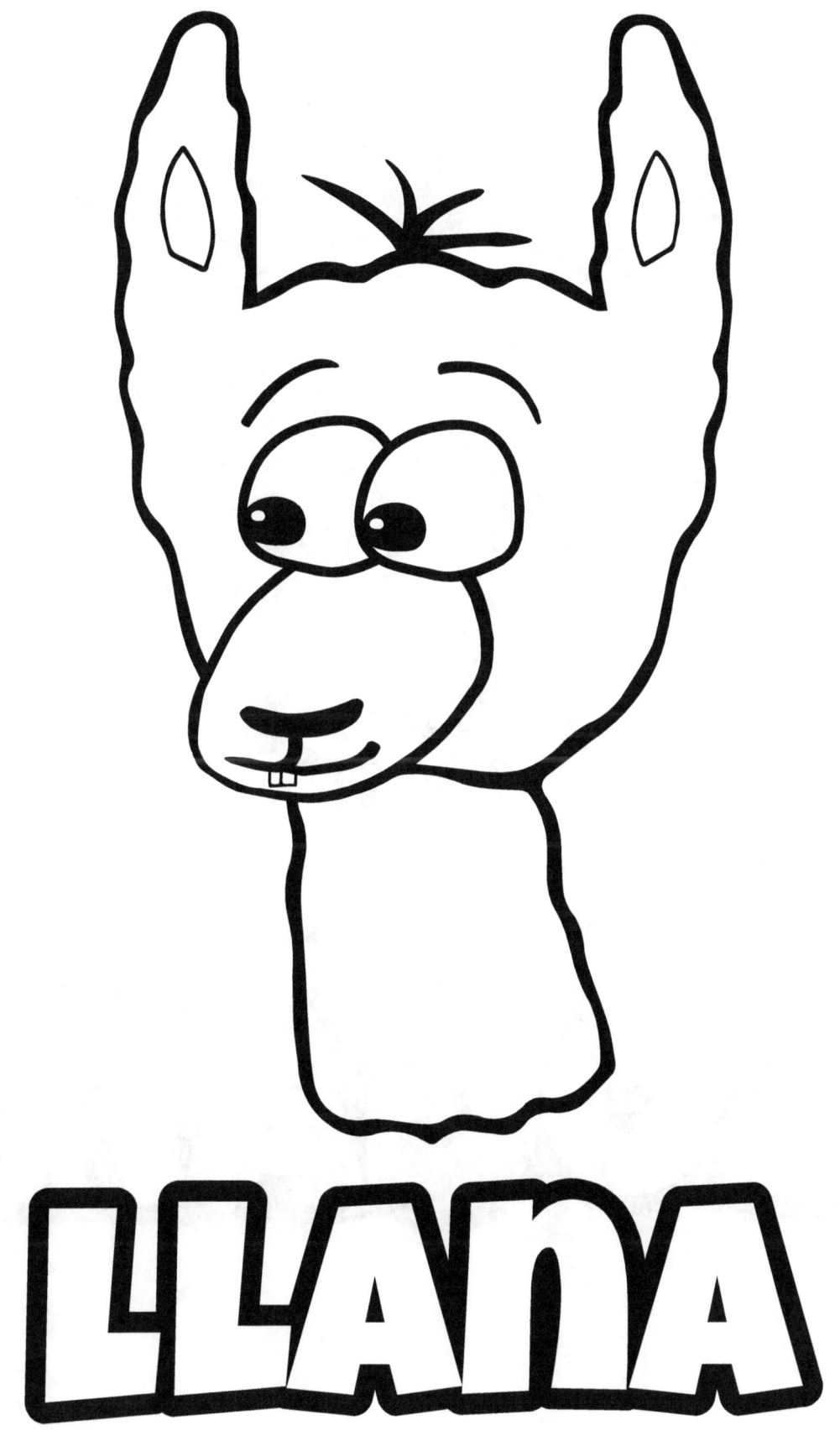

LLANA

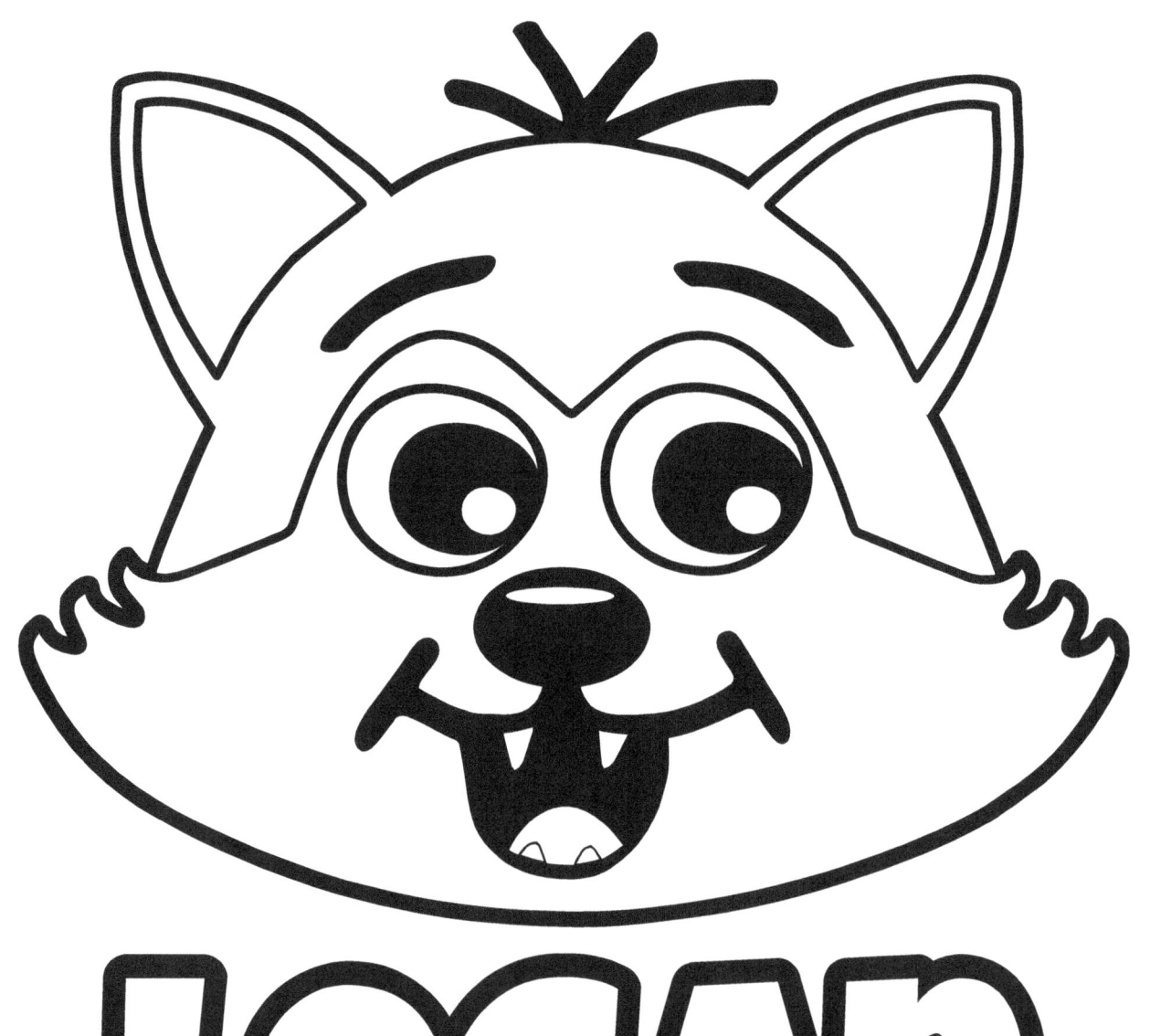

LOGAN

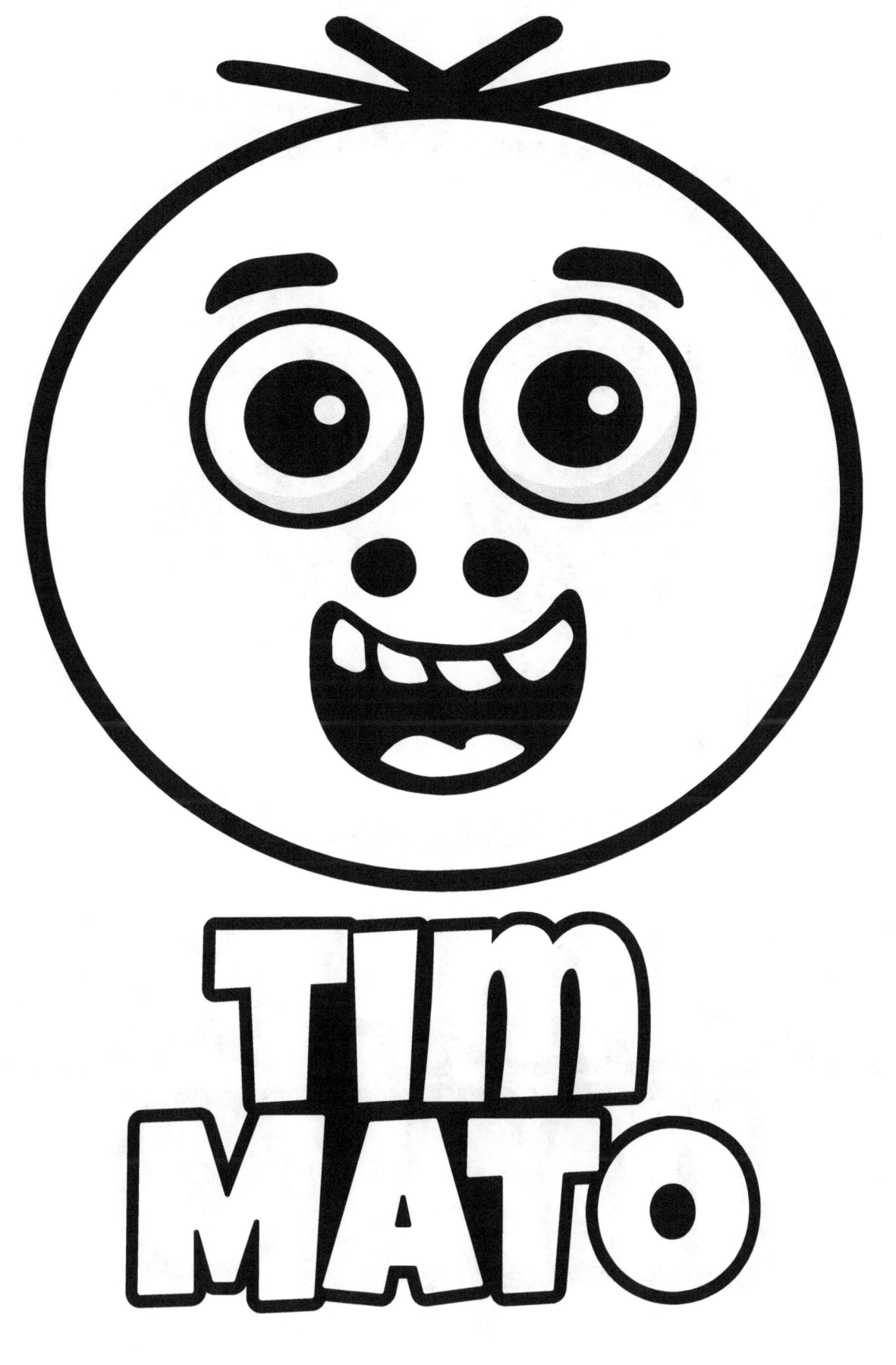

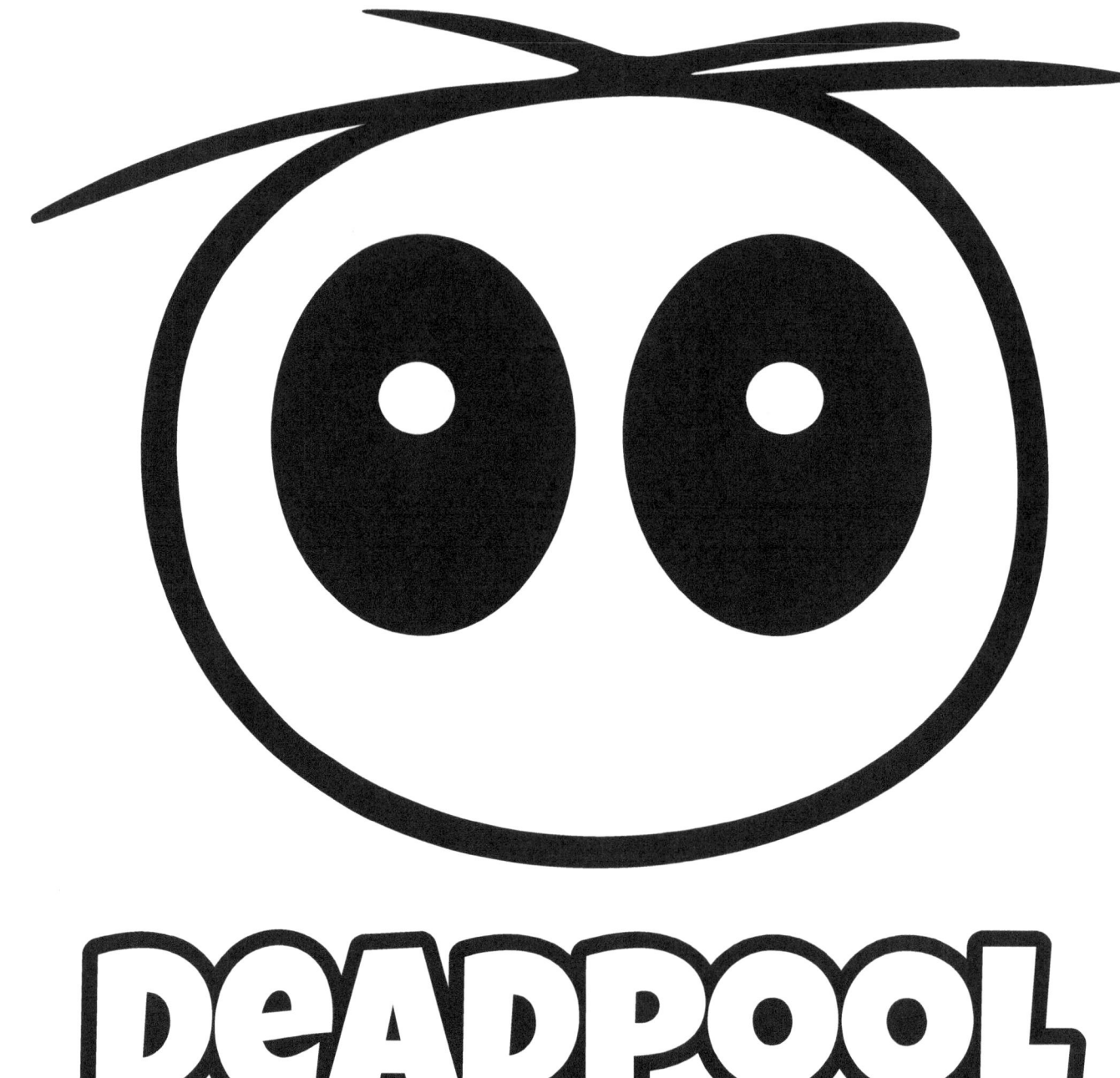

DEADPOOL
MATO

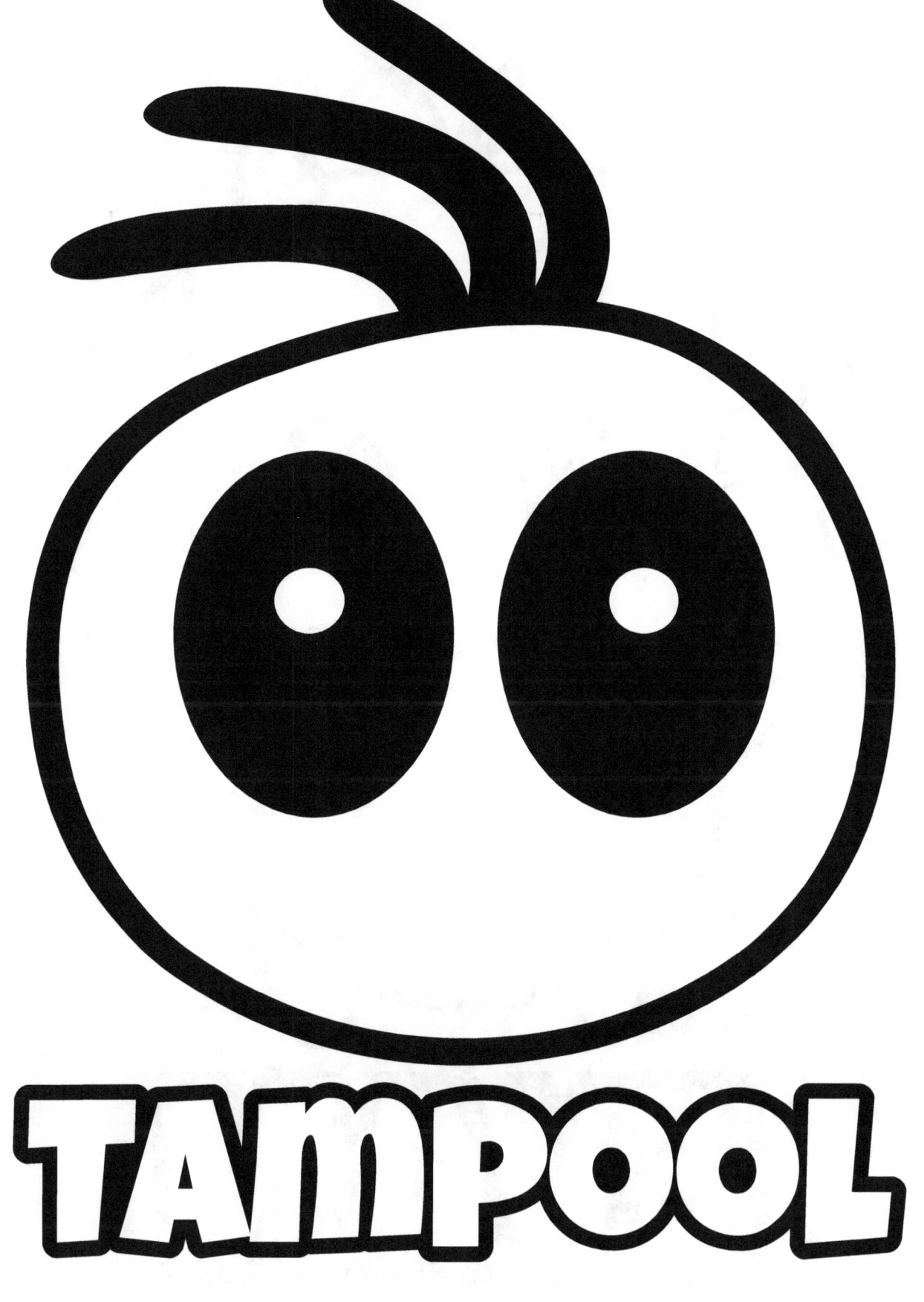

TAMPOOL

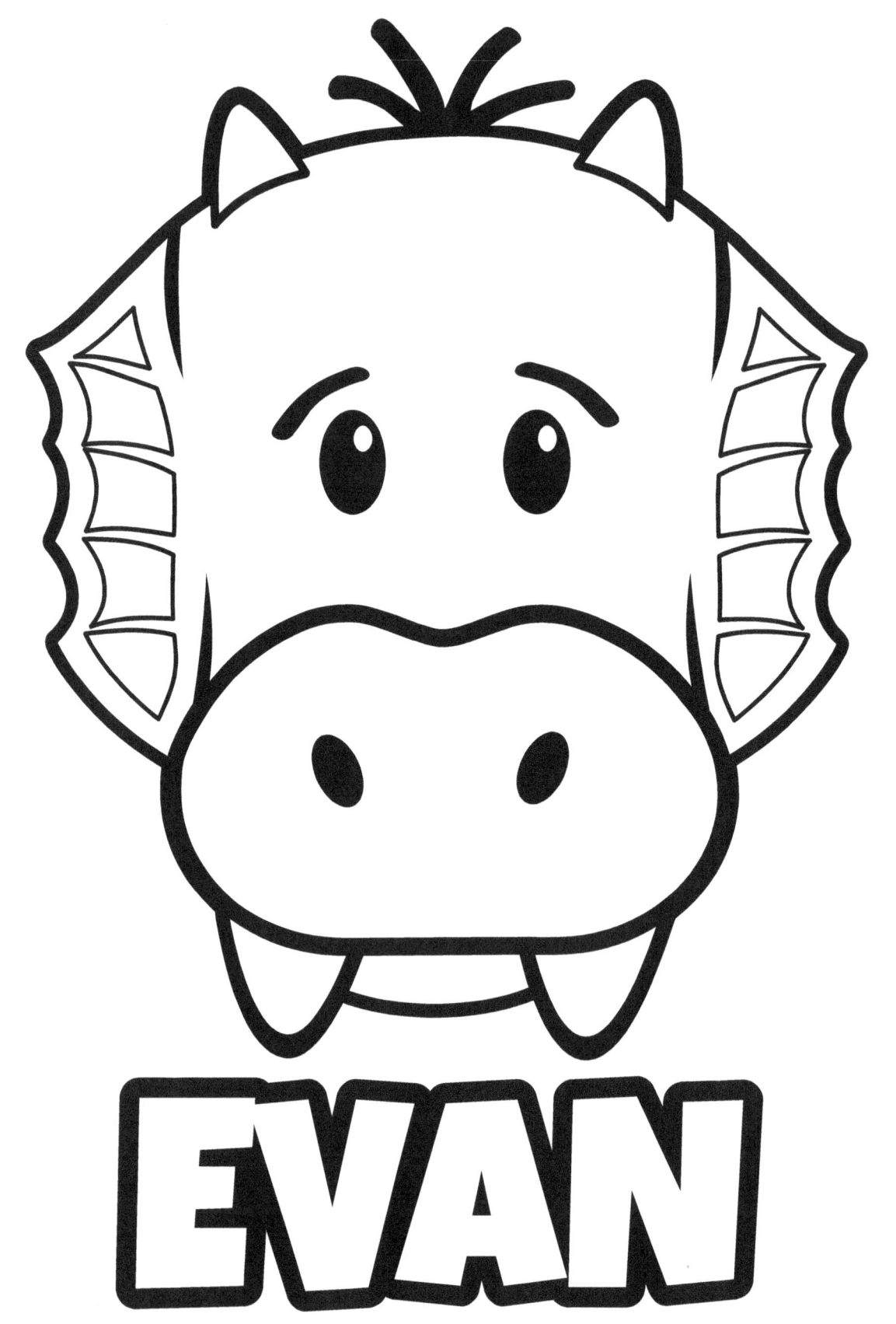

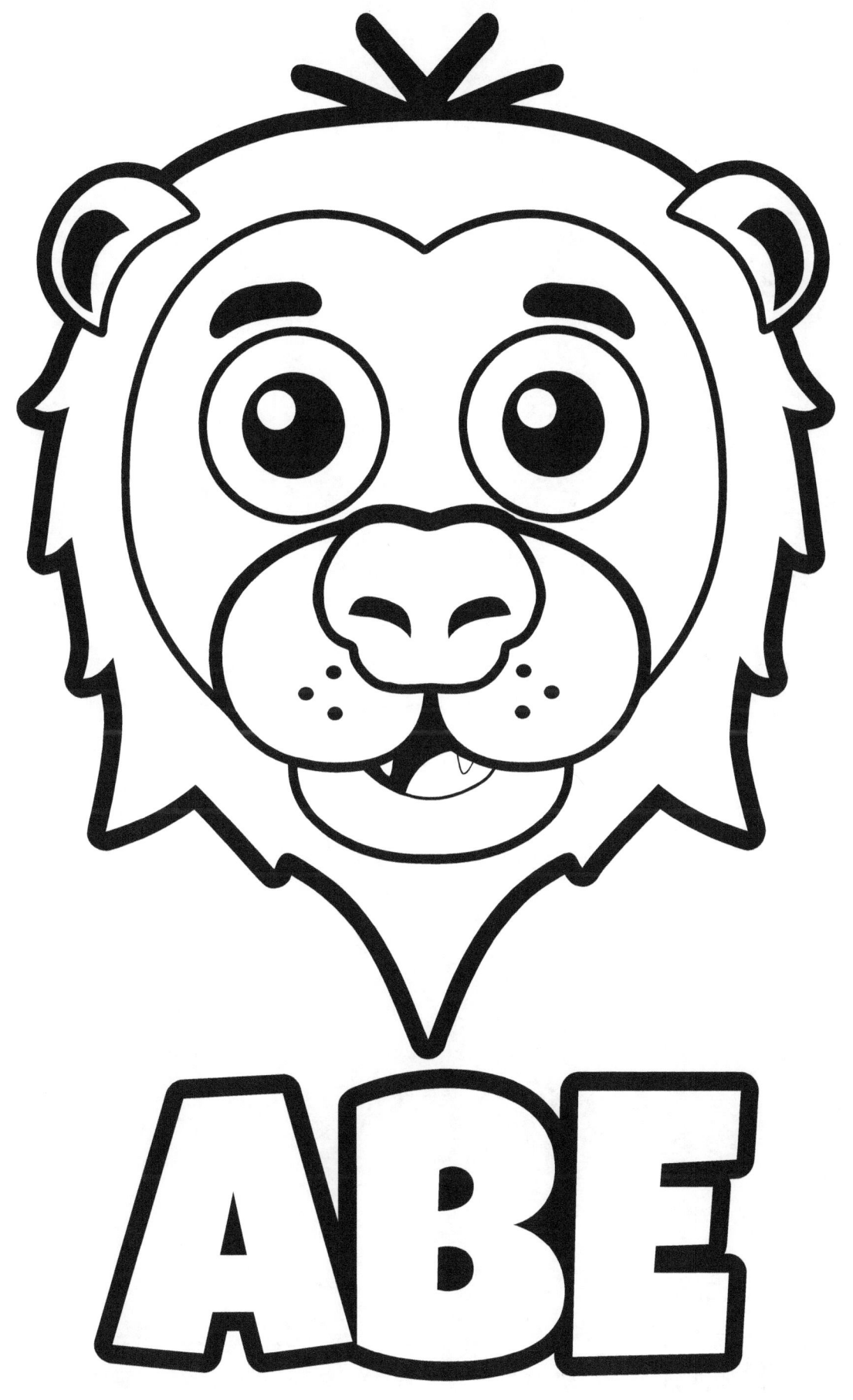

ABE

www.ingramcontent.com/pod-product-compliance
Lightning Source LLC
Chambersburg PA
CBHW080552190526
45169CB00007B/2737